THE NEW SPAIN

THE NEW SPAIN
From Isolation to Influence

Kenneth Maxwell

and

Steven Spiegel

COUNCIL ON FOREIGN RELATIONS PRESS

NEW YORK

COUNCIL ON FOREIGN RELATIONS BOOKS

If you would like more information about Council publications, please write the Council on Foreign Relations, 58 East 68th Street, New York, NY 10021, or call the Publications Office at (212) 734-0400.

Library of Congress Cataloging-in-Publication Data

Maxwell, Kenneth, 1941–
    The new Spain : from isolation to influence / Kenneth Maxwell and Steven D. Spiegel.
        p.   cm.
    Includes bibliographical references and index.
        ISBN 0-87609-163-X : $14.95
    1. Spain—Politics and government—1975–   I. Spiegel, Steven II. Title.
DP272.M39   1994
946.083—dc20   93-44751
                                                                           CIP

94   95   96   97   EB   10   9   8   7   6   5   4   3   2

Cover design: Michael Storrings

CONTENTS

PREFACE

We have aimed in this book to provide a concise introduction to one of Europe's greatest success stories of the past two decades: the making of the new Spain. After half a century marked by civil war and dictatorship, Spain is now a full member of the European Community and is a model for peaceful democratic transition. Discussion of democratization tends to swing from euphoria to gloom. After the fall of the Berlin Wall and the demise of the communist regimes in Eastern Europe and the former Soviet Union, many observers failed to reckon with the difficulties ahead. Yet today we may well overemphasize the obstacles. The transition on the Iberian peninsula followed a similar pattern. Spain had a regime of the right, to be sure; yet it also had elements of a market economy in place. It was part—if imperfectly—of the West. But some saw the ground as infertile to democracy, and much of the modern history of Spain served to encourage gloomy prognostication.[1] So the success of democracy here is not without wider significance, as the Spaniards themselves have been quick to point out. Yet Spain's example is not limited to the establishment of a successful democratic regime. Since the mid-1970s Spain, a "nation of nations," as some have described it, has also had to devise a solution to the complex problems of containing nationalisms with a state structure, and to do so within a democratic framework. It has not succeeded completely in this task, as the continuance of Basque terrorism shows; nevertheless, its solutions are worth considering in the post–Cold War environment, where such problems have become endemic. And finally, Spain has successfully removed the military from the political arena, something many of Spain's former colonies in Latin America have been unable to achieve.

We have attempted to describe in clear and straightforward terms how this remarkable transformation occurred in a narrative that we hope will be accessible to a wide range of interested readers. We have divided our analysis into four stages: the preconditions for democracy and the decomposition of the Franco regime; the transition of the 1970s; the consolidation of democracy under the Socialists during the 1980s; and finally, the new phase now beginning as a consequence of the 1993 general elections. Spain has attracted a good deal of interest among scholars, but its new role in international affairs and the depth of the changes which made this possible are still surprisingly unknown to many who are concerned with public and international affairs. We hope this book will help to remedy this deficiency and contribute to a wider appreciation of Spain's new democracy and its role in Europe and beyond.

ACKNOWLEDGMENTS

We are grateful to Nicholas X. Rizopoulos, Director of Studies at the Council on Foreign Relations, for encouraging us to transform a background paper from a Council symposium on Spain into a book, and to James Hoge and John Brademas for their careful reading and valuable comments. We have also benefited from the discussion of the participants in our symposium on Spain and the co-chairs of the event, John Brademas and Inmaculada de Habsburgo. We are especially grateful to Edward Malefakis, Angel Viñas, and Juan Antonio Yañez for their comments and criticisms. Appreciation is owed to the Rockefeller Foundation, whose generous grant to the Council on Foreign Relations made this project possible.

GLOSSARY

AP: *Alianza Popular* (Popular Alliance)

CAP: Common Agricultural Policy (of the European Community)

CC OO: *Comisiones Obreras* (Communist trade union)

CDS: *Centro Democrático y Social* (Democratic and Social Center party)

CEOE: *Confederación Española de Organizaciones Empresariales* (Spanish Employers organization)

CiU: *Convergéncia i Unió* (Catalan nationalist party)

CSCE: Conference on Security and Cooperation in Europe

CSCM: Conference on Security and Cooperation in the Mediterranean

EC: European Community

ECU: European Currency Unit

EMS: European Monetary System

EMU: Economic and monetary union

ERM: Exchange Rate Mechanism (of the European Monetary System)

ETA: *Euzkadi Ta Askatasuna* (Basque terrorist organization)

GDP: Gross domestic product

GNP: Gross national product

GRAPO: *Grupo Revolucionario Antifascista Primero Octubre* (Left-wing terrorist organization)

ICF: Interterritorial Compensation Fund

IU: *Izquierda Unida* (United Left party)

LOAPA: *Ley Orgánica de Armonización del Proceso Autonómico* (Law for the Harmonization of the Autonomy Process)

NATO: North Atlantic Treaty Organization

OECD: Organization for Economic Cooperation and Development

PCE: *Partido Communista de España* (Spanish Communist Party)

PNV: *Partido Nacionalista Vasco* (Basque Nationalist Party)

PP: *Partido Popular* (Popular Party)

PSOE: *Partido Socialista Obrero Español* (Spanish Socialist Workers' Party)

UCD: *Unión Centro Democrático* (Union of the Democratic Center party)

UGT: *Unión General de Trabajadores* (Socialist trade union)

WEU: Western European Union

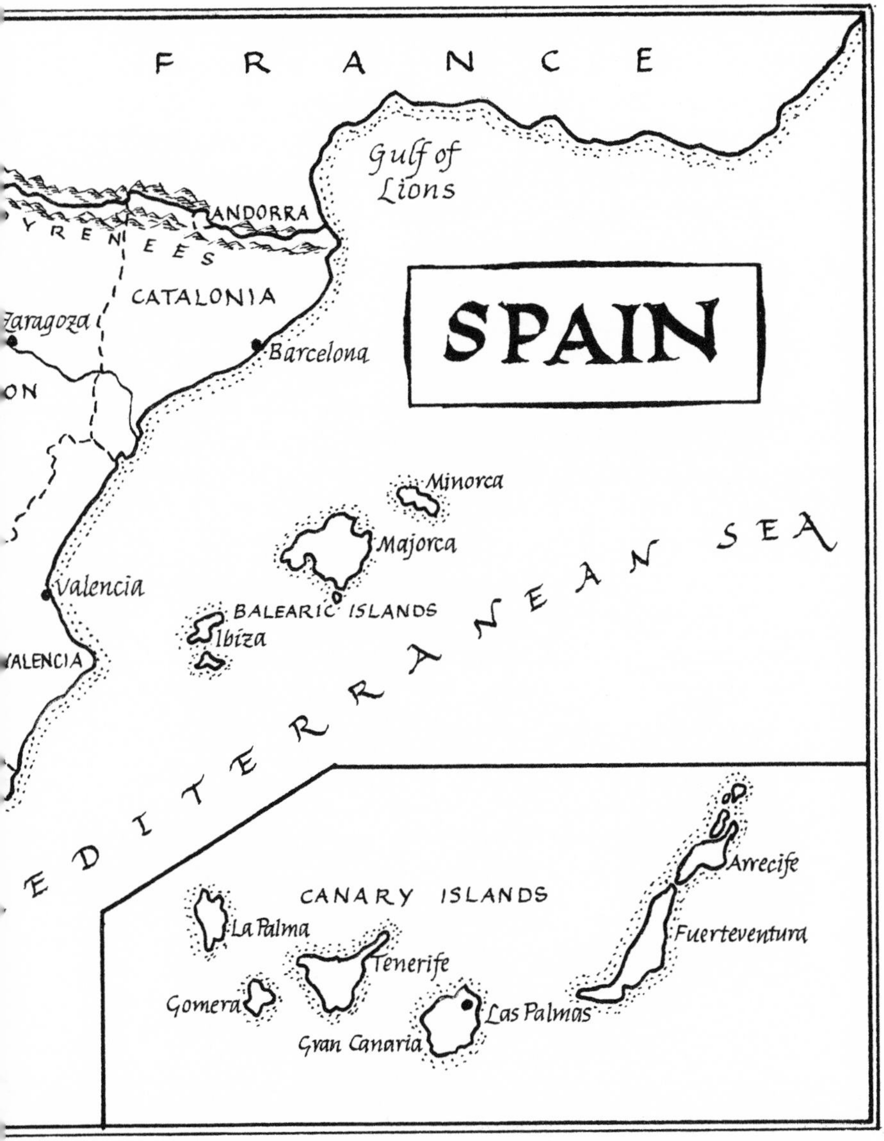

FRANCE
Gulf of Lions
ANDORRA
PYRENEES
CATALONIA
Zaragoza
Barcelona
SPAIN
Minorca
Majorca
BALEARIC ISLANDS
Ibiza
Valencia
VALENCIA
MEDITERRANEAN SEA
CANARY ISLANDS
La Palma
Tenerife
Gomera
Gran Canaria
Las Palmas
Fuerteventura
Arrecife

Chapter 1

INTRODUCTION

On June 6, 1993, the people of Spain went to the polls in the fourth general election since the promulgation of the democratic Constitution of 1978. In a result that surprised many in the media who had predicted a defeat for his Socialist party, Prime Minister Felipe González Márquez retained the largest bloc in the Cortes (parliament) and was called upon by King Juan Carlos I to form a government. The period since the Socialists first took power in 1982 has been marked by the full integration of a once isolated Spain into the community of nations— most importantly, as a significant partner within the European Community (EC) since 1986, but also as a North Atlantic Treaty member, and an active participant in United Nations peacekeeping activities and the Security Council. Domestically, Spain has rapidly modernized its infrastructure and industrial policy. Its vibrant cultural and social life again merits recognition as one of Europe's most creative and significant. Historical antagonisms between Spain and its former colonies, especially within Latin America, have been superseded, and Spanish diplomats, businessmen, and academics are now fully part of any transatlantic dialogue. So much so, in fact, that the historian Edward Malefakis has claimed that "Spanish prestige abroad is higher now than at any time

1

in the past 200 years."[2] All these are signs of a successful, self-confident, and democratic Spain.

But the outcome of the 1993 general election, the dissension that preceded it within the ruling Spanish Socialist Workers' Party (PSOE), and the need for coalition building by a leadership used to a majority position in the Cortes are likely to produce a period of uncertainty. After an interval of considerable success, Spain's Socialist government suffered several setbacks in 1992 and 1993. The peseta came under severe attack in the fall of 1992, and the government was forced to realign Spain's currency three times within the exchange rate mechanism (ERM) of the European Monetary System (EMS); in the runup to the second devaluation alone, the Bank of Spain spent almost one-third of its reserves to defend the peseta. Financial scandals and accusations of corruption also tarnished the Socialist party. Finally, long-simmering divisions within the PSOE, primarily over economic policy—between deputy party leader Alfonso Guerra and his supporters and the government's economic policy team, led by Finance Minister Carlos Solchaga—became all too obvious to the general public.

Yet despite these difficulties and the crushing defeat in March 1993 of the French Socialists, Felipe González was able to paste over intraparty differences in the late spring and moved quickly to call a general election before the summer recess.

The race was close and difficult, with many undecided voters waiting until the last moment. Yet González beat back the challenge of a revived conservative opposition and in a personal triumph garnered sufficient seats in parliament to embark on an unprecedented fourth term as the leader of Spain's government. But the challenges ahead on the economic and political fronts are formidable. How has Spain accomplished this remarkable political, economic and social transformation since the death of Franco, and what are the country's prospects for the rest of the 1990s?

Chapter 2

THE TRANSITION TO DEMOCRACY

The dramatic social and economic changes that occurred during the later years of the Franco regime were important preconditions to the establishment of a democratic regime in Spain. Today, these changes are so commonplace that it has become fashionable to remark how ordinary Spain has become; how like other European countries; how it is as if Generalisimo Francisco Franco (1892–1975) had never existed. But it is a mistake to forget so quickly what Spain was and how far it has come since 1975.

ECONOMIC AND SOCIAL CHANGE UNDER FRANCO

According to an old adage attributed to Talleyrand, "Europe ends at the Pyrenees." Even in the mid-1970s the aphorism held some truth. Spain had not been involved in World War II, and in this respect, with the exceptions of its neighbor Portugal and the traditionally neutral nations of Sweden and Switzerland, it was unique in Europe. One important consequence of non-involvement in World War II was that Franco's regime incorporated many holdovers from the European right-wing authoritarianism and fascism of the 1920s and

1930s, elements eliminated elsewhere in Europe as a result of the victory of the Allies. Franco had been helped to power by Nazi Germany and Fascist Italy, and his legislation to control and direct the press and the labor unions was borrowed directly from Mussolini.[3]

By the early 1960s, however, Franco had mitigated the harsh dictatorship of his early years. As the Spaniards said, the *Dictadura* (hard dictatorship) had become a *Dictablanda* (soft dictatorship). This change was largely a consequence of economic development and the desire for international respectability. At the time, the true dimensions of this transformation were often discounted. The origins of the Franco regime in a bitter civil war (1936–1939), a war that many saw as the opening battle of World War II, were never forgotten either by Franco and the defeated republicans or by the international forces on the right and left that the Spanish conflict mobilized. And although Franco imposed peace, his personality allowed little room for "forgiveness." Thus, the political parties of the republic, especially the Spanish Socialist Workers' party (PSOE) and the Spanish Communist party (PCE), existed clandestinely throughout the Franco period, many of their leaders living in exile. As a devoted centralist, Franco also vigorously repressed expression of non-Castilian nationalism within Spain, especially in Catalonia and the Basque provinces.

Franco created a structure of constitutional laws and a corporatelike parliament intended to embody the principles of "organic democracy," in contrast to what the theorists of corporatism regarded as the artificial "inorganic democracy" of universal suffrage, political parties, and a government responsible to an elected parliament. His philosophy was explicit in traditionalism and autocracy, which were in many respects more important components of the regime than were the more overtly fascistic elements borrowed from abroad. Franco was strongly anticommunist. In time his hostility to liberal democracy was muted, especially after the defeat of the Axis in 1945, while his anticommunism became more virulent, particularly after the beginning of the Cold War in 1947. This shift of emphasis was in part tactical and incorporated no espousal of democratic values, since Franco to the end remained firmly committed to the basic tenets of his system.

Despite this political immobility during the 1960s, the "Spanish miracle" dramatically modernized Spain's conservative and rural society through urbanization and industrial development (see Table 1).[4] In 1950, 50 percent of the active population of Spain was engaged in agriculture; by 1970 the figure was 29 percent. A massive exodus from the countryside occurred. In 1950 Spain had 3 million unskilled farm laborers; by 1970, only 986,000.[5] The industrial work force grew in the same period from 2.5 million to 4 million.

These changes had been in part the result of Franco's abandonment in 1959 of a policy of economic autarchy. In February of 1957 he brought into the government a team of able young technocratic ministers (Alberto Ullastres, Minister of Commerce, and Marianno Navarro Rubio, Minister of Finance) and the more experienced Laureano López Rodó (head of the Technical Secretariat of the Presidency of the Government), who drastically restructured Spain's approach to the government's economic role: in 1959 they adopted a stabilization program linked to economic liberalization, and in 1963 they devised a strategy based on national economic planning. The series of development plans Franco's technocrats set in motion in the early 1960s also benefited from the mitigating of Spain's diplomatic isolation and the overall European boom, in which Spain

TABLE 1. MEASURES OF SOCIAL AND
ECONOMIC CHANGE IN SPAIN

	1960	1970	1980	1991
Total population (millions)	31	34	38	39
Gross National Product per capita ($)	375	872	4,100	13,500
Birthrate (per 1,000 population)	22	20	15	11
Infant mortality (per 1,000 live births)	44	28	10	8
Employment (percentage of total):				
Agriculture	42	29	18	11
Industry	31	37	36	33
Services	27	34	46	56

Sources (relevant volumes): World Bank, *World Development Report*; OECD, *Economic Surveys of Spain*; and Keith G. Salmon, *The Modern Spanish Economy* (London: Pintar, 1991)

was able to participate.[6] The key diplomatic events in Spain's political reintegration into the international system were the 1950 UN resolution lifting economic and diplomatic sanctions, the 1953 concordat with the Holy See, the 1953 defense agreement with the United States (Pact of Madrid) and membership in the UN in 1955, and in the OECD, World Bank, and International Monetary Fund in 1958.[7] As a consequence of these institutional changes, the economy grew rapidly in the 1960s and 1970s. Between 1959 and 1964 per capita income increased by about 9 percent per annum, industrial production and capital formation by over 10 percent. By 1980 Spain was the eleventh-leading industrial nation in the world.

Spain's convergence with the norms of West European consumer society was rapid, and between 1960 and

1975 real per capita income tripled. In 1960 only 4 percent of Spanish households owned a car; by 1970, 12 percent did; by 1977, 51 percent. The proportion of households with television sets rose from 32 percent in 1966 to 90 percent in 1977.[8]

One important consequence of economic development was stronger links with the rest of Western Europe. Spain became the recipient of large capital inflows as a result of mass tourism, as well as the export of workers who, once established in France or West Germany, remitted large sums to family and dependents at home. During 1978 the total number of tourists in Spain reached 40 million, more than Spain's population of 37 million.[9]

Within Spain, the impact of social and economic changes, especially on behavioral patterns, was substantial. The burdens of these transformations were also soon apparent: chronic traffic, congestion, and pollution in once sleepy cities; housing shortages; and generational tension over social mores. The beneficiaries of Spanish development, however, were surprisingly many, with small businesses thriving in the service sector and in construction. Overall, Spain witnessed the growth of a substantial middle class, the rise of an impressive generation of young technocrats, and the expansion of broad social security coverage and access to education. With migration and development, Spain also saw an increasing scarcity of labor, which in turn gave workers considerable strength in their relationship with employers.

In the process, the old Francoist labor framework was eroded. By the 1960s new Communist-inspired *comisiones obreras* (workers' commissions) were organized on a national scale and engaged in extensive strike action. The number of working hours lost through strikes rose from 8.7 million in 1970 to 14.5 million in 1975. This exercise of power resulted in real gains. Wages and salaries rose to 63 percent of the net national income by 1975. Spanish industrialists tacitly accepted a process of collective bargaining, in effect abandoning the regime on this important component of the Francoist state's social vision and institutional arrangements for labor-management relationships. This development does not imply that repression lessened. On the contrary, between 1968 and 1973 at least 500 workers' leaders were imprisoned.[10]

During and after the Civil War, the Catholic church had been strongly committed to Franco. But with time this close mutual embrace became increasingly embarrassing to Rome and to a large portion of the Spanish clergy. The church in Spain, especially after the reign of Pope John XXIII, distanced itself from the regime. Even this modest shift had dramatic implications. For historical reasons, the church in the Iberian peninsula had always stood with the authoritarian right and had no discourse with the traditionally anticlerical liberals and the left. The shift in the church's position, therefore, helped heal one of Iberia's most persistent and bitter cleavages.[11]

In education also, change was dramatic. University enrollment in 1941 in Spain had been 37,000. By 1961, the number of students had risen to 76,000. In the 1960s enrollment nearly tripled; it stood at 229,000 in 1971. By 1970 about 90 percent of all children in Spain were receiving primary education, compared with 50 percent twenty years before.[12]

To be sure, the increasing economic and social approximation to Western Europe carried some disadvantages. If Spain was able to benefit from Europe's boom, it also became vulnerable to Europe's economic recession. The shock of the 1973 rise in oil prices and the world recession that followed had a severe impact on the

West European economies, immediately affecting access of Iberian labor to the EC countries. Totally dependent on imported petroleum, Spain was extremely vulnerable to increased energy costs.[13]

There were also impediments to full integration into the European mainstream despite Spain's social and economic change. In the end the delay in full integration with Western Europe was largely attributable to the longevity of Franco himself and the legacy of the Civil War he represented, although 70 percent of the Spanish population was under forty in 1975 and thus had no memory of the tragic struggles of the 1930s.[14]

THE TRANSITION FROM FRANCO

In the early 1970s, President Richard M. Nixon, concerned about what might happen when Franco died, sent General Vernon Walters, who had served on many occasions as his translator during delicate negotiations, on a private mission to ask the old Caudillo what he had planned for Spain following his demise. Franco told Walters that there was no need for alarm; he had created institutions, the army would be loyal, and the transition would be smooth.[15]

On this last point Franco was more right in his prediction than were his enemies, who, if they predicted anything for Spain following Franco's death, predicted chaos.[16] In the other assertions, however, Franco could not have been more wrong. Therein lies the paradox: a liberal constitutional regime evolved from the shell of the dictatorship itself; Franco's "institutions" dissolved themselves.

Democratization in Spain took place by consensus and reconciliation. The new system incorporated the previously clandestine anti-Francoists and the opposition accepted important continuities from the Franco era—especially in the security and military area. Initially the transition was conducted by a broad but factious centrist coalition, the Unión de Centro Democrático (UCD), led by Adolfo Suárez, a former functionary of Franco's political movement.

King Juan Carlos appointed Adolfo Suárez to the presidency of the government (the official title of the Spanish prime minister is *presidente del gubierno*) on July 3, 1976. Suárez successfully opened an unprecedented dialogue with the center and the left, with the objective of moving toward national elections that would be recognized as fair and honest by all sides of the political spectrum as rapidly as possible. He also facilitated the formation of a competetive electoral vehicle for the center, fostering the integration of the multitude of small political parties and factions that had emerged in Spain following Franco's death into the Union of the Democratic Center (UCD). Suárez also contributed decisively to the pact-making between the political parties that lay behind the successful constitution-making negotiations and the agreements on economic and social policy during the critical transition period.

Although the UCD achieved remarkable breakthroughs in constitution making and institutional innovation, it was increasingly unable to contain its centrifugal balances, and chose to postpone difficult decisions about the economy and the implementation of the new constitution in the spirit of compromise and social peace during the process of political democratization. Six developments explain some of the special features of Spain's democratization.

First, King Juan Carlos I played an instrumental role in consolidating democracy. The king, as Franco's designated successor, provided continuity. Crowned in

November 1975, King Don Juan Carlos de Borbón is a grandson of Spain's last ruling monarch, Alfonso XIII. Franco personally selected Juan Carlos to succeed him in preference to his father, Don Juan, the pretender, who was well known for his liberal views. Unlike the proverbial Bourbon who "forgets nothing and learns nothing," King Juan Carlos (b. 1938), despite the careful education he had received under Franco's direct supervision, was well aware of the disparities between Francoist Spain and the West European mainstream. Upon Franco's death, to the surprise of most observers, Juan Carlos placed his prestige firmly behind the new democratic institutions and acted with considerable political deftness behind the scenes during the transition. During the critical year of 1976, he skillfully steered through the Francoist Cortes the dramatic Law for Political Reform, which by stipulating the immediate dissolution of the legislative body, in effect invited the Cortes to abolish itself. Moreover, the king backed the construction of the broad centrist UCD coalition which was critical to the transitional period, and worked closely with Suárez. Spain's first free democratic election, in 1977, was the fulfillment of the reform program the king had initiated.[17] Thus, the role of King Juan Carlos I was unique to Spain. He used the quasiauthoritarian powers granted to him as Franco's designated successor to implement reform initiatives, divested himself of his powers, and assumed the largely ceremonial role of constitutional monarch in a parliamentary democracy.[18]

The second significant development in the democratization of Spain was the emergence of the strong, moderate, and majoritarian PSOE as a major competitor for power. Within the PSOE a young generation of leaders, including Felipe González and Alfonso Guerra, faced down maximalist demands from the rank and file in 1979 and transformed the PSOE into a moderate party on the Western European social democratic model. This allowed the party to drop much of its Marxist baggage and concentrate on electoral politics. The move increased the party's popularity and propelled it into the government in 1982.[19]

Third, Spaniards were aware of the failures of the republican regime of the 1930s and built mechanisms into the Constitution of 1978 to impede the fall of the government.[20] Parliament delegated the writing of the Constitution to a broadly based but small group of experts who worked in total privacy and placed compromise high on their agenda. As a consequence, the Spanish Constitution, with the important exception of its treatment of the Basques, is universally accepted and does not stand in the way of programmatic decisions by the government. Pact making was critical to Spain's success by involving the unions, the church, business, and political parties from the left and the right, thus creating an atmosphere conducive to constitutional negotiations and to restructuring the economy.[21]

Fourth, two symbols of past polarizations, the church and the Communist party, had moved toward the center of the political spectrum. Santiago Carrillo, the Spanish Communist leader, became a leading exponent of Eurocommunism, had broken with the Soviet Union, and embraced a parliamentary path. The church, for its part, had embraced democracy and, more important, provided no legitimacy for the enemies of democracy, as it had often done historically.[22]

A fifth significant development is the external factor: Spain almost totally avoided international intervention or interference in the 1970s. Here again the king was reassuring, going out of his way to guarantee the Americans, most notably in a speech before a joint session of the U.S. Congress in 1977, that a democratic Spain was not a threat, but a realization of their democratic aspirations. The American presence in Spain was not popular, but the United States was not there as an occupation force, nor had it been involved in actions to repress freedom. The U.S. presence, though resisted, was in no way comparable to that of the Soviet army in Eastern Europe. The democratization of Spain moreover marked the removal of an obstacle to its full and active participation in Western multinational organizations.

Although negotiations and compromise were preeminent characteristics of the transition from authoritarianism, the outcome of Spain's institutional engineering was radical and marked a clear break with the immediate past—a point about Spain's democracy that has almost always been overlooked. The constitutional monarchy established in 1978 is a system entirely different from the one Franco set up. On the other hand, Spain's social and economic transformation had been incremental and had occurred in the two decades before Franco's death. Raymond Carr, the great British historian of modern Spain, has long argued that in the past Spain sought to impose advanced institutions of representative government on an archaic social structure, with results that were almost always disastrous and often bloody.[23] By the 1970s, however, Spanish society had changed: it had become modernized, consumer-oriented, capitalistic, moderate, and middle class. Yet this vibrant new Spain was overseen by superannuated institutions. The transition to democracy reconciled the long-standing differences between institutions and society, but the social changes and the political skill that made democratization possible may be unique to Spain.

CIVIL-MILITARY RELATIONS

There was a counterpoint to this steady process of liberalization that, through provocation aimed essentially at the army and the security forces, was intended to derail the process. Terrorism was a constant element in the political equation, both before the death of Franco and afterward. In September 1975, two months before the generalisimo's demise, five terrorists convicted by a military court of killing policemen were executed despite widespread public opposition in Western Europe. In December 1976, the terrorist organization Grupos de Resistencia Antifascista Primero de Octubre (GRAPO) kidnapped the president of the Council of State only days before the referendum on political reform. In January 1977 GRAPO kidnapped the president of the Supreme Council of Military Justice; on the same day ultra-rightists murdered four of the Communist party's lawyers at their Calle Atocha office in Madrid. Both kidnap victims were rescued, but terrorism continued to threaten Spanish institutions through the whole period of transition and, linked as it is to separatist aspirations, continued to plague the young democracy.[24]

It should be remembered that the armed forces had helped create Franco's dictatorship. Franco's army was, after all, an institution that had grown from the nationalist forces victorious in a civil war. Therefore, in many parts of Spain, the army had been traditionally one of occupation, and its deployment (especially the placing of armored brigades near the major cities) reflected the dictates of the government's internal security concerns more than external defense. The Spanish armed forces in 1977–1978 numbered 309,000 (217,000 conscripts); the paramilitary forces (Guardia Civil) and Policía Armada numbered 65,000 and 38,000 respectively. Defense expenditures in 1977–1978 were $2.15 billion. In 1980 the Spanish army had 565 generals, most of them over the age of seventy-three, the youngest near sixty.[25] On February 23, 1981, elements of the army and the paramilitary security forces attempted to overthrow the new constitutional democracy. This attempt was the most sensational manifestation of a deeper process of change and adjustment.

During the dramatic years from the death of Franco in 1975 until the aborted coup of 1981, the Spanish army stood moodily on the sidelines as institutions of the old regime were eradicated and the new Constitution was put in place. The Portuguese revolutionary experience of 1974–1975, when the fall of dictatorship led to a rapid radicalization of the political scene and the emergence of a strong left-wing faction within the military, was a salutary one for the military in Spain at this time. The Portuguese precedent served to strengthen the reformers within the military who saw a civilian, constitutional regime as a way to achieve major changes within the military that they wished for and, indeed, had largely articulated before the death of Franco. These reformers, aware of the king's close relationship with the military, welcomed change. They were entirely unsympathetic to what was broadly and unflatteringly referred to as "the bunker" (the old-line Francoists).

Yet rumblings of discontent within the armed forces continued over questions such as the legalization of the Communist party in 1977, the explicit recognition in the 1978 Constitution of the multinational and multilingual character of Spanish society, and the murder by the terrorist organization Basque Nation and Liberty (ETA) of the commanding officer of the army's most important division, as well as of other officers and policemen.

Discontent came to a head when, at 6:25 P.M. on February 23, 1981, Lt. Col. Antonio Tejero and his supporters in the Guardia Civil seized the Cortes building during parliamentary proceedings on the confirmation of Leopoldo Calvo Sotelo as prime minister, holding the government and the parliament hostage. Concurrently, Lt. Gen. Milans del Bosch, military commander in Valencia, declared martial law and brought his troops into the streets to take control of the city. Tejero and Bosch were acting on a traditional view held by the military that when the political class was unable to tackle difficult problems—in this case Basque terrorism and regional questions—it was the duty of the military to intervene.

The main lesson of this critical juncture, was the invaluable role played by the king, consolidating his position as constitutional monarch in a country that had been badly divided for most of the twentieth century between monarchists and republicans. King Juan Carlos I had above all provided a clear focus of authority and continuity and became central to protecting democracy under challenge. He responded with emphatic support for the existing constitutional order and, through discussions with key military commanders, rallied the support of the military. King Juan Carlos made clear to the conspirators that he would neither support the coup nor abdicate. For seven hours the standoff in parliament continued. Finally, at 1:24 A.M. the king appeared on national television in his uniform as commander-in-chief of the armed forces and declared that "the crown . . . cannot tolerate in any form actions or attitudes of persons who try to interrupt the democratic process of the Constitution." With the army's official support, the coup ended peacefully within a matter of hours when Tejero surrendered.

Although the effect was not immediately apparent, the coup attempt furthered the consolidation of democracy and galvanized a public that had been lulled into taking its new democratic institutions and freedom of expression too much for granted. Several days after the failed coup, more than a million people demonstrated in Madrid in a rally for democracy; similar rallies attracted over 300,000 people in Valencia and 200,000 in Barcelona. But the political class also became aware of the need to modernize the military establishment and to seek the collaboration of the military in doing this. The military was able to pressure the government to pursue new policies toward terrorism and regionalism. There was an implicit agreement that the government had a moral commitment to maintaining the unity and territorial integrity of Spain; in June 1981 a parliamentary commission provided a structure for the reorganization of autonomous regions with designated powers of self-government, and in July 1981 the government enacted the Law for the Harmonization of the Autonomization Process (LOAPA).

Spain was fortunate perhaps in that it faced no serious external threat during the course of democratization. The country had sensibly avoided the risk of a debilitating foreign military involvement during the mid-1970s, again by the king's instigation, by rapidly withdrawing from the potentially explosive situation in what was the Spanish Sahara.

There was, of course, a major internal threat from terrorism, associated principally but not exclusively with the continuing crisis in the Basque Country, where a substantial proportion of the population wanted greater autonomy than had been granted so far, and a minority wished for outright independence. According to one 1984 survey, 44 percent of young Basques continued to believe that violence was an acceptable means of promoting Basque national interest.[26] Paradoxically, this terrorist threat facilitated the integration of the security and intelligence services of the old regime into the new democratic structures, since the existence of the terrorist threat helped legitimize the security services and paramilitary forces and preserve an important continuity in these institutions. Since terrorism did not diminish with the end of the Franco regime, these forces, which otherwise would have been scrutinized and perhaps dismantled, soon became essential to the defense of the democratic state.

Naturally, ambiguities emerged; these institutions had been bastions of the dictatorship and still harbored individuals with decidedly undemocratic values. The conciliatory nature of the Spanish transition also served to incorporate a large sector of the Francoist bureaucratic apparatus into the new system. Yet it is important to note that public opinion approved the task of defending democracy from assaults, and this approval helps explain the lack of retribution against the security services that had long sustained Franco's rule. That is almost unique in the course of change from an authoritarian to a democratic regime and stands in marked contrast to the fate of PIDE, the secret police in Portugal, or the Stasi in East Germany.

The failed coup of 1981, moreover, had the beneficial effect of forcing the undemocratic elements within the armed forces into the open. Before 1981 civilian politicians and the press had been highly circumspect, even fearful, with regard to talking openly of plotting within the military. After 1981 this became a major item of discussion and press exposure. In other words, mysterious forces that had been frightening were identified and no longer seemed threatening. The result was greatly to diffuse the threat from the unreconstructed right.

CENTRALISM AND REGIONALISM

Spain was and remains a country of diverse nationalities. A constant theme in modern Spanish history has been the oscillation between a rigorous centralism and accommodations between Madrid and the nationalist minorities within the Spanish state. The old dictatorship, and the defeated republic before it, had to face the issue. For the new constitutional monarchy, the challenge of how to deal with Basque nationalism created a problem requiring the greatest statesmanship. The Suárez government had moved quickly to respond to the aspirations of Spain's two most active nationalities, the Basques and the Catalans. It granted considerable power to autonomous regional institutions. In September 1977 the Catalan Generalitat was reestablished, and in December the Basques also received substantial autonomy from Madrid. Between December 1979 and February 1983, Madrid extended autonomy to all the Spanish provinces (see Table 2), creating an increasingly complicated mosaic of quasi-federated regional governments (see Map 1).[27]

The initial problem facing the new regime in Spain was thus less structural (in the economic and social sense) than it was related to the difficult, age-old Spanish problem of the contradictory pull of authority and democracy within a multinational state. The government in Madrid must mediate between the demands that press on the Spanish state from the now institutionalized autonomous regions and the powerful presence of "national" institutions not encompassed (or left untouched) by the transition to constitutional monarchy—for example, the military, the church, and the financial and banking sys-

TABLE 2. DATE OF APPROVAL OF STATUTES OF AUTONOMY
FOR AUTONOMOUS COMMUNITIES

AUTONOMOUS COMMUNITY	DATE OF APPROVAL
Basque Country	December 18, 1979
Catalonia	December 18, 1979
Galicia	April 6, 1981
Andalusia	December 30, 1981
Asturias	December 30, 1981
Cantabria	December 30, 1981
La Rioja	June 9, 1982
Murcia	June 9, 1982
Valencia	July 1, 1982
Aragon	August 10, 1982
Castilla—la Mancha	August 10, 1982
Canary Islands	August 10, 1982
Navarre	August 10, 1982
Balearic Islands	February 25, 1983
Castilla y León	February 25, 1983
Extremadura	February 25, 1983
Madrid	February 25, 1983

tems. Spaniards themselves made the point by distinguishing between what they call *poderes fácticos*—that is, "real" power, or power of fact—and the legal, or constitutional, system.[28]

Partly because of this tension, the politicians who played key roles in the transition period found administering democracy to be more difficult than establishing it. Adolfo Suárez, in particular, proved weak, hesitant, and unprepared for leadership when faced with a more populist political environment, while being subject to crushing pressures from those whose interests and well-being were tied to the state's actions or interactions. This was especially true with respect to the financial and industrial elite. The role of the banks, for example, was central to the welfare of the large industrial concerns. In the 1960s, for instance, seven of the 112 banks in Spain managed 70 percent of all foreign resources, granted 60 percent of all loans, held 90 percent of all private assets, and controlled a quarter of Spain's 200 largest industrial enterprises.[29] During the period of transition, this symbiosis of the financial world, the civil service, and the government brought some advantages—in particular, it was an important lever for implementing the government's policy of social and economic stabilization—but it also gave rise to some of the less-savory episodes of financial scandals and manipulations in recent Spanish history.

The UCD government under Suárez also had difficulties dealing with more overt economic problems—a 25 percent inflation rate and an unemployment rate over 10 percent. Moreover, a key part of the national consensus that had created the UCD and made it a success also disintegrated. The ad hoc, makeshift nature of the coalition itself—embracing people of quite liberal persuasions with old-line Christian Democrats and conservatives—brought endemic factionalism and backbiting, and the party remained dependent on its control of government apparatus instead of strengthening and developing its grass-roots support.[30] The church hierarchy, a firm supporter of "transition" as a general good in itself, parted company with the centrists over the specifics of social policy, coming out forcefully against the legalization of divorce, something Suárez himself strongly supported.[31] The military also began increasingly to exert behind-the-scenes pressure against what it regarded as a dangerously escalating dismemberment of Spain through the compromises (capitulations, in the army's view) worked out between the UCD government and regional autonomists. This period also saw an escalation of terrorist violence (see Figure 1), much of which was

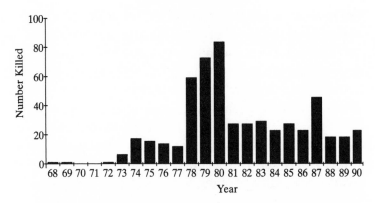

FIGURE 1. DEATHS FROM TERRORIST VIOLENCE 1968–1990

Reprinted from: *Politics, Society and Democracy: The Case of Spain*, Richard Gunther, ed. (1993) by permission of Westview Press, Boulder, Colorado.

directed against the military. Facing what he saw as impossible conditions for effective leadership, Suárez resigned on January 29, 1981. Parliament was in the process of selecting Suarez's successor when elements of the paramilitary Guardia Civil staged the coup attempt of February 23, 1981.

Leopoldo Calvo Sotelo, Adolfo Suarez's successor, had some victories. With broad multiparty support, a new law for the defense of the Constitution, aimed principally at the continuing terrorist challenge, gained approval. On the economy, the Calvo Sotelo government was able (also in mid-1981) to reach a labor agreement setting wages below the inflation rate. In a break with the consensus politics practiced until then, the new government precipitously decided that Spain should join the North Atlantic Treaty Organization (NATO), a decision that created much controversy and engendered loud dissent from the major opposition party, the Socialists.

The internal factionalism of the UCD continued, moreover, and the prime minister seemed helpless against it. In addition, many believed that the Calvo Sotelo government had behaved with undue deference in its relations with the military. The verdicts after the long court martial of the would-be coup-makers seriously affected only the two leaders; the other conspirators escaped with minimal sentences.[32] Military policy, moreover, often appeared to be dictated to the government by the armed forces themselves. Right-wing officers openly sneered at the democratic institutions, even at the king, and were barely reprimanded.[33]

In addition, the government found that the political repercussions of elections in the newly autonomous regions strengthened their opponents on the right (as evidenced by the victory of Manuel Fraga Iribarne's Alianza Popular in Galicia) and on their left (hence the overwhelming victory of the Socialists in Andalusia).[34] The desertion of the moderate Catalans in early 1982 left the government in a minority and placed its survival in the hands of Socialists, who were able, in effect, to choose the timing of the general elections to suit their own strategy and to deny this advantage to the incumbents. The election of October 1982 confirmed what the opinion polls had been predicting for some time—a victory for PSOE and an overall majority of seats for the Socialists in parliament.[35]

Chapter 3

THE CONSOLIDATION OF DEMOCRACY

Since 1982 the Spanish central government has been dominated by the Socialist party under the leadership of Prime Minister Felipe González. Under his guidance Spanish democracy was firmly consolidated, major economic reforms were implemented, the military was modernized and placed under civilian control, the relationship with the United States was made more equitable, and Spain joined the EC. Against the background of these achievements Spain moved dramatically to assert a new role in Europe and on the world stage.

THE SOCIALISTS IN POWER

Throughout the period of democratic transition, the Spanish Socialists were in opposition. The PSOE was able to take advantage of this breathing space for important learning experiences within its organization and in relationship to the functioning of the new system. Thus, although the Socialists participated in all the pacts and agreements that made democracy possible in Spain, they did not bear responsibility for the failures of the UCD government.[36]

Without question, the peaceful transfer of power to the first Socialist government to hold office since the turbulent years of the Second Republic marked a re-markable affirmation of the strength of Spanish democracy. The leader of the PSOE, Felipe González, became prime minister. González, a forty-year-old lawyer from Seville, was untested in government; yet he very soon proved himself to be one of Europe's most dynamic and attractive politicians. His tenacity and dynamism was critical to ensuring the success of Spain's democratic transition. The transformation of the PSOE into a major political organization, however, was largely the work of Alfonso Guerra, the deputy leader of the party, who had been a close friend to González since the early 1960s when they rebuilt the Andalusian section of the PSOE together. In effect, Guerra fulfilled the role of Machiavelli, while González was the prince. They proved a formidable combination during a decade of Socialist rule. Above all, the arrival of the Socialists in power marked a profound generational shift as a younger, more cosmopolitan leadership group moved into positions of authority.[37]

In the 1982 general elections the PSOE took 40 percent of the popular vote and 202 of the 350 seats in parliament, allowing the Socialist party to form a single-party government, and giving Spain the first strong majoritarian government in its parliamentary history. The socialists acted pragmatically in office and were reelected for a second term in 1986. In 1989 the PSOE lost majority control of the Congress of Deputies by one seat. But González returned to office and won a vote of confidence because of the absence of four Basque deputies. Table 3 shows results of the 1977–1993 general elections.

A corollary of the continuity achieved between the old regime and the new during the transitional period was that Spain retained a strong central government, despite the parallel phenomenon of the creation of au-

TABLE 3. SEATS IN CONGRESS OF DEPUTIES FOLLOWING
GENERAL ELECTIONS

	1977	1979	1982	1986	1989	1993
PSOE	110	121	202	184	175	159
UCD/CDS	166	168	13	19	14	0
CiU	11	8	12	18	18	17
PNV	8	8	8	6	5	5
AP/PP	16	9	107	105	107	141
PCE/IU	19	23	4	7	17	18
OTHERS	20	13	4	11	14	10

PSOE—Spanish Socialist Workers' Party.
UCD—Union of the Democratic Center. Name changed to CDS in 1989
   election.
CiU—Convergence and Union (Catalan nationalist party).
PNV—Basque Nationalist Party.
AP—Popular Alliance. Alianza Popular (AP) led electoral coalitions in 1979,
   1982, and 1986. Name changed to Partido Popular (PP) in 1989.
PCE—Spanish Communist Party. PCE formed leftist coalition Izquierda
   Unida (IU) beginning with the 1986 election.

tonomous regional governments throughout the territory. The state's strength soon helped the PSOE, with its
large parliamentary majority, to achieve a quasihegemonic
control over the poorer regions, which depended on the
central government's largess. Unlike Portugal and many
of the former communist states of Eastern Europe, where
the nomenklatura retained considerable power even after the transition to democracy, the Socialists were able
to take command of the bureaucracy quickly. This cap-
ture of power and of the political center had the effect of
limiting the area in which any extremist political vision—
either of the right or the left—could easily be articulated.

For example, the Communists, despite the role their
party played in negotiating the democratic transition,

reaped few benefits from the process. In fact, the party fragmented and was subsequently largely marginalized. The Spanish Communist party, in contrast to its Portuguese counterpart, did not challenge the Socialists as an electoral force in any way. The party gained little from its espousal of Eurocommunist doctrines; on the contrary, Eurocommunism fragmented the party, and lost it the support of the Catalan Communists (PSUC), who opposed Eurocommunism as heresy. Many of the party's leading intellectuals, on the other hand, did embrace Eurocommunism and insisted this also means internal party democracy, as well as rhetorical support for constitutionalism and moderation. The Socialists were also able to develop a strong union base, the old Socialist-controlled General Union of Workers (UGT), rivaling the Communist-dominated *comisiones obreras* in terms of worker allegiance.[38]

The public, in any case, wanted moderation and Europeanization above all else. Those who wanted to return to the past, particularly disgruntled military officers, had little influence after 1981–1982. The emergence of the strong, moderate, and governing Socialist party was likewise an important development within Europe, distinguishing Spain from Italy or Portugal whose Socialist parties have been unable to achieve a similar hegemony on the left.[39]

Once in power the Socialist government moved aggressively to improve and expand Spain's infrastructure, especially its roads. Attention was given to education reform, cultural affairs, and social policy, including the legalization of abortion. Above all, the Socialists confronted the chores left unfinished during the transitional period: the reform and professionalization of the military, the normalization of international relations, and the modernization of the economy. These were the tasks of securing and consolidating the democratic gains of the 1970s, and they marked the second major phase in the construction of the new Spain.

MILITARY REFORM

After the electoral victory in 1982, coming as it did shortly after the failed coup of 1981, the Socialists made military reforms a major political objective. Significantly, they placed at the head of the Ministry of Defense a Catalan politician and former mayor of Barcelona, Narcís Serra Serra, who had developed a good relationship with the military before the Socialist victory. Serra established civilian control, reoriented budget and deployment provisions, and embarked on a major effort to modernize the Spanish military, reorienting the army's role away from internal security and toward national defense.

Despite the coup attempt and perhaps in some ways because of it, the process of establishing civilian control of the armed forces has been surprisingly rapid and successful. The Ministry of Defense was a relatively recent innovation, dating only from 1977, and reflected the desire of reformist officers for internal modernization of the armed forces, as well as the need by civilian politicians to establish the primacy of civil over military power in decision making. When the Socialist government came to power in 1982 and began implementing the reform of the armed forces, therefore, it found some effective collaborators among high-ranking, reform-minded officers in all three services and a basic institutional structure in place. Previously, the UCD had excluded the military from the constitution-making process, and the relationship between the armed services and Adolfo Suárez was often tense. Military leaders complained that they heard of measures affecting them from the mass media, not from the government itself. The Socialist government embarked on its reforms in an incremental manner and with broad consultation.[40]

The Socialists had three major objectives: to bring Spanish defense structures more into line with those of Western Europe; to professionalize and streamline the armed forces; and to make Spain more independent of foreign arms supplies by encouraging domestic suppliers. Modernizing these structures was a more radical process than it might first appear. In the mid-1970s the Spanish military, especially the army, resembled a Latin American force more than a NATO army, with an elderly and bloated officer corps and 62 percent of its budget spent on personnel (compared with 43 percent in West Germany and 40 percent in Great Britain). In early 1984 the government modified the defense law to give the prime minister greater authority over command and coordination of the armed forces. In this he was to be advised by the National Defense Board and a reformed Joint Chiefs of Staff. The joint chiefs now became a consultative, not a command, body.

The 1984 amendment also increased the powers of the minister of defense, who became responsible for overall military policymaking. In 1985 promotion and appointive power was concentrated in the hands of the chiefs of each service and the minister, and a new position of chief of the general staff was created, with responsibility for joint action of the services. These and subsequent reforms gave real decision-making power to the Ministry of Defense, which used this power thoroughly to overhaul defense planning and to set priorities for force size and the acquisition of materiel. The army suffered the heaviest burden of change. A phased 16 percent reduction in the number of army officers was initiated, and reductions of 8 percent were imposed on the navy and air force. By 1991 the number of active military personnel had been reduced sharply from 285,000 in 1988 to only 217,000 (158,000 of whom are conscripts)—and the term of conscription had been reduced from one year to nine months. As of 1990, Spanish defense spending stood at roughly $7 billion, or 2.4 percent of gross national product (GNP).

At the same time as these major organizational changes were getting under way, equally important shifts occurred in the system of military justice, limiting the extensive powers military tribunals had exercised during the Franco era. In 1984 the Socialist government adopted a "joint strategic plan" that defined the overall objectives of the armed forces in the new democracy. These consisted of defending the constitutional order, guaranteeing the territorial integrity of Spain, protecting the population from aggression or natural disaster, committing to the defense and security of the Western world, and establishing effective control over the Strait of Gibraltar and its approaches. The practical consequences of these preoccupations—especially concerning the Maghreb—were the strengthening of the southern military region and the Naval Combat Group based at Rota, and the deployment of F-18As. Of course, the lack of specificity about the Soviet threat in Spanish military planning in the 1980s allows the Spaniards to claim with some justification that they were prescient in their view of East-West relations.

Overall the process was one by which the Spanish armed forces were becoming—in the words of a former chief of the defense staff, Adm. Angel Liberal Lucini—"like those in any other Western country."[41]

NATO AND THE AMERICAN ALLIANCE

Three conditions influenced the evolution of the Socialist government's foreign and defense policies in the 1980s. First, Spain had to surmount the constraints of its historical experience. Second, the Iberian region underwent a process of Europeanization. Third, the Atlantic connection, involving bilateral relations with the United States, was subject to substantial modification. In each instance, priorities were reordered.

Curiously, although the process of democratization in Spain received a great deal of scholarly attention and a substantial literature now exists on the subject, the interaction of the new regime with the rest of the world has been little studied. Given that events in Spain were of central concern during the immediate prewar period, and that widespread interest in the Spanish Civil War continues among the general public, this is worthy of note, because one of the little-noted reasons for the success of the move from dictatorship to democracy was precisely that Spain avoided outside interference and the East-West controversy during the critical years of transition. However, other important legacies from the Franco period needed to be overcome before Spain could attain its full place within the European and international communities.

In many respects Spain had been marginal to the European mainstream since the end of the Napoleonic wars, and for almost fifty years, principally as a result of the Civil War and the nature of the Franco regime, Spain had played an insignificant role in international affairs. Spain did not share the modern industrialized nations' formative influences and experiences, such as participation in World War II, in postwar reconciliation and economic reconstruction, and in the building of European transnational institutions. Indeed, until the early 1950s Spain was formally excluded from the new international organizations. Even in the early 1970s, a large part of the international community regarded Spain as a pariah. This exclusion limited what Spain could do internationally, and the Spanish elites' exposure to international experience. Thus, for many decades the country's international relations were severely distorted and self-limiting.

The beginning of the Cold War brought about a rapprochement with the United States. Spain was firmly anticommunist, and that, more than anything else, helped it to develop close security relationships with Washington after 1952. But Iberian anticommunism, coming from the interwar decades, was accompanied by a hostility to the postwar Western community's democratic values, and the dissociation of "defense of the West" from "defense of Western values" implied by the defense agreements between Franco and the United States was not without repercussions during the transition period of the 1970s and early 1980s. The anti-Franco forces' feelings of betrayal because of these security arrangements, in particular, were at the root of Spain's difficulties in integrating foreign and defense policy into a coherent and popularly acceptable doctrine after the establishment of the new regime. One of the most controversial tasks of the new democracy thus became to develop a defense and foreign policy more in keeping with a democratic polity and Spain's importance within Europe.

Spain's process of normalization of international relations was marked by its accession to NATO in 1982, to the EC in 1986, and to the Western European Union (WEU) in 1988. For Washington the nature of bilateral relations under Franco provoked some ill will over the U.S. bases in Spain after democratization. In Spain, however, the diminution of the U.S. presence was seen as providing an array of options that in no way undermined Spain's basic engagement in a democratic Europe. In retrospect it is ironic, given the internal opposition to Spain's joining NATO and the lack of resonance that talk of the "Soviet threat" had among the Spanish public, that Spain's belated entry into the Western alliance occurred on the eve of shifts in the international system so profound as to bring into question the very basis of NATO, or at least its rationale as an anti-Soviet coalition.

The peculiarities of Spain's post-World War II political situation particularly affected the Socialists. The Socialists viewed the cozy relationship between the United States and Franco, including the deals to permit U.S. bases in Spain, as Franco's abnegation of Spanish sovereignty and Washington's condoning of Franco's dictatorship.[42] Until the mid-1970s the PSOE had been a clandestine and to a large extent exiled organization. Thus, partly for historical reasons, the party's connection with the French Socialists was strong; from 1975 on, the supportive role of West Germany, and the Social Democratic Party (SPD) in particular, was also important, especially via the SPD's Friedrich Ebert Foundation and the trade unions.[43] This conduit provided advice, money, and organizational expertise.[44] On the other hand, until 1976 the United States had no official relationship with the Spanish Socialists, although the PSOE had informal contacts with individual Americans. These contacts tended to be part of the old republican network; they were influential in transatlantic left and intellectual circles, but they were weak in official connections. The PSOE's views of America therefore tended to reflect the position of opponents of U.S. administrations and, more generally, of the counterculture of the 1960s and early 1970s.

Wells Stabler, who was ambassador in Madrid during the most critical years of the transition, decried the lack of preparation in Washington for the inevitable demise of Franco. Without precise instructions as to what would happen, Stabler was surprised when President Gerald R. Ford's visit to Madrid was announced in 1975. Since Franco was then eighty-two years old, Stabler saw no reason for the presidential visit. Many Spaniards asked Ford: "Why do you have to do this? What do you gain from it?" The fact was, according to Stabler, that the "visit achieved absolutely nothing at all except, again from Franco's point of view, indicating that the big friend was rallying around."[45]

Washington's indifference, though generally benign, did not go unnoticed in Spain, and many—especially Socialists—interpreted it as hostility to democratic aspirations. At the time of the attempted coup in 1981, the Spanish press reported that U.S. Secretary of State Alexander Haig described the assault on the parliament as "an internal matter." This further damaged bilateral relations, especially with the already suspicious left. In 1985, on the eve of an official visit to Madrid, President Ronald Reagan spoke of the Abraham Lincoln Brigade, which had fought in defense of the republic against Franco: "I would say that the individuals that went over there were, in the opinion of most Americans, fighting on the wrong side." This comment raised a particularly unfortunate memory of U.S. hostility to the republican cause in the 1930s, a cause in which Franco's supporters included Hitler and Mussolini and the republic's supporters had included the PSOE. Spanish ministers, among them Prime Minister Felipe González, went out of their way thereafter to emphasize to American audiences that they saw the history of the 1930s in a different light. The participation of Americans in the International Brigades, González told a meeting at the Woodrow Wilson Center in Washington, D.C., in November 1986, mitigated America's embrace of Franco's dictatorship. The sensitivity of Spanish Socialists to foreign-policy issues—particularly American faux pas—also grows from the fact that these issues had the potential of mobilizing the grass roots of the party in a way that could embarrass the leadership.

Ironically, Spain under Franco had been excluded from NATO precisely because of Western sensitivities about its regime (although such sensitivities had not applied to Spain's smaller but no less dictatorial neighbor Portugal, or to Greece under the colonels). Yet the historical legacy of Western engagement with Franco made the question of Spain's joining NATO especially sensitive.[46]

In a break with the consensus policies followed throughout the transition period, the decision by the centrist government of Leopoldo Calvo Sotelo to join NATO was highly controversial. The decision was motivated at least as much by political objectives as by security needs. In fact, after the 1981 coup attempt, some saw participation in NATO as a means of keeping the army out of domestic politics. Public opinion, however, was unprepared for this change. According to opinion polls, the Spanish people did not feel threatened by the Soviet Union and tended to worry more about the potential for conflict in the Mediterranean and with Morocco over the Spanish enclaves of Ceuta and Melilla. The Socialists fought their victorious election campaign in 1982 with an anti-NATO plank and a pledge to hold a national referendum on NATO membership. Spanish public opinion also remained especially skeptical about U.S. intentions. In a 1984 poll on NATO, a request for an opinion about the U.S. bases received a 70 percent negative result; among PSOE voters, the negative result was 76 percent.[47] Asked on the eve of President Reagan's visit in 1985 if "the U.S. and its president are loyal and sincere friends of Spain," only 13 percent of the general public agreed; 74 percent disagreed.[48]

Under considerable international pressure and with the NATO issue increasingly linked to Spain's application for EC membership, however, the Socialists, once in government, shifted positions. Having won the 1982 election, the Socialist government moved hesitantly to fulfill its pledge of a referendum on NATO, delaying it until March 1986. Realizing that NATO membership was critical to Spain's integration into the Western community, González campaigned vigorously in support of continued NATO membership.[49] In a reversal of his earlier antagonism, González argued that "to break our relations with the Atlantic Alliance would create a trauma, with consequences I cannot foresee."[50]

In spite of opinion polls predicting an anti-NATO victory, the Socialists won the NATO referendum with 52.6 percent of the vote, but with the inclusion of a clause calling for the reduction of American military personnel in Spain and a prohibition on the storing or installation of nuclear weapons on Spanish territory.[51] The negotiations on U.S. base rights that followed were acrimonious and led to the forced withdrawal of the U.S. Air Force 401st Tactical Fighter-Bomber Wing from Torréjon, outside Madrid.[52] The U.S. Navy, though, maintains a deployment of 3,400 personnel at the Rota naval base. As Felipe González told his American audience frankly at the Woodrow Wilson Center on September 27, 1985, "Americans and Spaniards must try to understand each other better, within a framework of mutual respect and friendship, which does not, however, exclude dissent when it is a matter of defending our own legitimate interests.[53]

The conflictive nature of Spain's reintegration into the international system on the geostrategic front stood in marked contrast to the public and political response to Europe, especially the EC, which the new Spain viewed as a model for economic prosperity and democratic politics. Europe was an aspiration, and with Franco gone, full membership in the EC was the goal of all Spanish governments following the installation of a parliamentary constitutional monarchy. In 1975, King Juan Carlos in his first public address reminded the rest of Europe that "the idea of Europe would be incomplete without a reference to the presence of the Spaniards and without consideration of the activity of my predecessors. Europe should reckon with Spain, and we Spaniards are European!"[54] No major sector of opinion in Spain doubted that the future lay in that direction.[55]

Spain's desire to join the EC dates back to Franco's request for negotiations with the Community in 1962. However, this bid was denied because of European hostility toward the undemocratic Franco regime. Following years of arduous negotiations, though, the EC and Spain reached a preferential trade agreement in June 1970 that called for mutual tariff reductions and the removal of quotas on 95 percent of EC industrial imports from Spain subject to tariffs, and 62 percent of agricultural imports; about 60 percent of Spanish imports from the Community were affected.[56] Spain applied for EC membership in 1977, following the death of Franco.

Having established democratic credentials, Spain expected to gain EC membership relatively quickly and easily. This was not the case, and the government felt considerable frustration with the resistance that emerged from the Community bureaucracy and from France. Following a two-year delay in the EC's acceptance of Spain's application, official negotiations for membership began in February 1979, and Spain expected to join the EC as early as 1982. Two main obstacles stalled the negotiations: Spain's agriculture and fishery sectors and Community financing. French and Greek farmers were fearful of competition from Iberian agriculture, and French farmers went as far as attacking Spanish trucks transporting agricultural products through France. Spain's accession would increase the EC's agricultural labor force by 25 percent, agricultural land by 30 percent, production of fresh fruit by 48 percent, and production of olive oil by 59 percent. These increases threatened existing EC producers by creating an excess supply of goods such as olive oil, fruit, and wine. A similar situation existed with regard to fisheries in that Spain, with the largest fishing industry in Western Europe, threatened the EC's fishermen. The tonnage of the Spanish fleet in 1986 was 70 percent that of the ten EC members (excluding Greece); after accession one-third of all EC fishermen would be Spanish.

The completion of negotiations with Spain was also delayed as the Community tried to resolve a contentious row over EC financing and the budget. In the midst of this battle, the EC bureaucracy feared the impact of Spanish accession on the Community budget, especially the effects of Spanish participation in the Common Agriculture Policy (CAP). Having resolved this dispute at the June 1984 Fontainebleau European Council meeting, the EC set January 1986 as the date for Spanish accession. Following an exhaustive eight-year round of negotiations, the Treaty of Accession was signed in 1985, but only after a last-minute attempt by Greece to derail the agreement. Spain (together with its Iberian neighbor, Portugal) officially gained full membership beginning January 1, 1986. Once Spain had achieved membership in the EC, it moved rapidly to play a full part in Community deliberations.

The accession agreement established a seven-year transition period during which Spain's integration into the EC would gradually occur. This transition period covered important areas such as the removal of customs duties and industrial tariffs on EC goods and the removal of Spanish import levies and most quotas. Longer-term arrangements, which would have expired in 1996, were made for the inclusion of Spain's agricultural industry in the CAP, and restrictions were established on fishery catches.[57] Membership in the European Monetary System was delayed until the Spanish government felt the economy was adequately prepared; Spain entered the system in 1989 with a wide exchange-rate band.

EC membership resulted in immediate economic benefits as the Spanish economy rapidly integrated with its EC partners. Between 1986 and 1990 gross domestic product (GDP) grew at a rate of more than 4 percent per year, and GDP per capita rose from $6,000 to $12,600. Spain's economy shifted dramatically toward the EC through expanded trade and investment. Between 1985 and 1990 Spanish exports to the EC rose from 52 percent of total exports to 71 percent; concurrently, imports from the Community rose from 37 percent of total imports to 60 percent. EC participation in foreign direct investment also climbed from 40 percent of total foreign direct investment in the period 1980–1985 to 57 percent in 1990.[58]

As the EC began to consider advancing to a new stage of integration, Prime Minister Felipe González became a leading supporter of greater integration and the Maastricht Treaty of December 1991. González has long supported the ideal of European unity and declared early in his career that "we must work in Western Europe with the idea of contributing to awaken once more the spirit of the 1950s, when European unity was an ideal that attracted the energies and enthusiasm of new generations."[59] He realized, though, that greater economic integration would require painful economic adjustment by the Community's poorer countries, including Spain, and he feared the Community would split into two tiers, leaving Spain in the second tier. González emerged as the leading spokesman for the poorer members, and he made increased financial support to the poorer Community members a sine qua non for support of the Maastricht Treaty. González obstinately challenged his EC partners, threatening to disrupt the process of European integration unless his demands were met.

After a long and often bitter struggle with Spain's wealthier EC partners, the issue of financing was settled at the December 1992 Edinburgh Summit, where González obtained a Community agreement to establish a "cohesion fund" benefiting only Spain, Portugal, Ireland, and Greece, and an increase in EC structural funds that would assist not only these countries, but all poor regions in the Community.[60] Over the period from 1993 to 1999, the cohesion fund will total about 15 billion European Currency Units (ECUs) of which 8 billion ECUs should go to Spain for investment in transport, telecommunications, and energy projects.[61] With other changes in the EC's budget, total transfers to these four states will nearly double to $46 billion by 1999.

González strongly believes in creating a federated Community and is committed to "deepening" the Community before "widening" it. He has been a vociferous supporter both of the formation of an economic and political union and of the resultant transfer of authority to Brussels. As he stated in an address to parliament, "To share sovereignty is the only way, the only solution to achieve this European Union."[62] Spain's commitment to deepening the Community was partially a response to fears of economic competition from the states of Central and Eastern Europe, and the Spanish government believed "deeper" European integration was a means of preventing the Community from diverting money and attention to these states. In any event, the Spanish parliament demonstrated its commitment to Maastricht by ratifying the treaty in October 1992—with only three members of the radical Basque party voting against—while other EC members continued to dawdle toward ratification. Moreover, frustrated by the slow progress made by other EC states, the Spanish government expressed its anger by threatening to delay ratification of the European Economic Area.

Yet while accession to the EC clearly benefited Spain in the second half of the 1980s, the pains of increased competition and necessary economic adjustment are beginning to catch up. As discussed below, the process of opening the economy to greater competition and the radical economic adjustment required to participate in European economic and monetary union are forcing Spain to swallow painful economic medicine. With all of Europe suffering through a serious economic recession in the early 1990s, the process of adjustment is all the more difficult.

THE SPANISH ECONOMY UNDER THE SOCIALISTS

The Spanish economic miracle ended suddenly in 1973–1974 primarily because of the oil crisis. GDP and

other key economic indicators plummeted. Inflation accelerated, foreign accounts became greatly imbalanced,
disposable national income declined, and profit rates
fell. The rise in petroleum prices strongly affected the
Spanish economy because Spain possessed a very poor
natural energy base, making it almost totally dependent
on petroleum imports, and the industries most affected
constituted an important part of the country's productive structure. The resulting economic crisis caused both
high inflation and high rates of unemployment. The
Spanish governments during the 1970s did little to adjust
the economy to the new economic reality of higher energy costs.

Even during the periods of rapid growth, the Spanish economy had remained heavily protected by high
tariffs and insulated from competitive forces, with large
state subsidies to inefficient industries. As the transition
to democracy began, the Spanish economy thus possessed many structural inadequacies: an entrepreneurial
class not accustomed to competition; a highly inefficient
state structure; and the production of excessive goods in
areas with limited domestic or international demand,
such as steel and shipbuilding. In addition, the Franco
regime made layoffs of workers very difficult—almost
impossible—and costly, creating a highly inflexible labor
force. It also maintained a financial system strongly
supported by a government system of price and production controls. In fact, it generally practiced economic
policies of central protectionism and interventionism
that encompassed most spheres of the Spanish economy.
The Franco regime maintained an inefficient, complex,
and highly regressive tax system, yet during the 1960s
launched a big social security program financed with a
payroll tax, which made labor costs even more expensive. Many state-owned firms—such as those in the Insti-

tuto Nacional de Industria, the state industrial holding company and the convalescent home for many Spanish industries that would have otherwise died under market pressures—operated with deficits, and these losses only intensified with the crisis.

These economic and structural rigidities remained largely concealed during the years of growth and economic expansion. They became, however, more obvious during the 1970s when magnified by the energy crisis.

The transition from the Franco regime to democracy was characterized by a period of consensus building which resulted in a series of political, economic, and social contracts: the Moncloa Pacts (1977), the Inter-Confederation Framework Agreement (1980), the National Employment Agreements (1981), and the Social and Economic Agreement (1984).[63] Important as these were to the political success of the transition period, they all possessed more political than economic rationale, and the centrality of political and social considerations served to delay Spain's economic adjustment.[64]

Once in power in 1982, the PSOE government acted more rigorously than its predecessor in attacking Spain's lingering economic problems. In this it enjoyed some advantages, to be sure. The PSOE possessed a strong parliamentary majority in 1982. Moreover, economic reforms were necessary or required for Spain's EC membership. Rationalization of key industries, taxation reform and the use of the value-added tax, and the reorganization of certain state companies were essential for Spanish membership and for competing successfully under Europe's economic rules and structures. Thus, the economic discipline necessary to make certain economic adjustments and structural changes was imposed from without. The PSOE government was also politically able to proceed with difficult economic decisions, such as industrial modernization, given the absence of a credible threat from its left. The devastation of the Communist party in the 1982 election meant that the PSOE government did not have to look over its left shoulder as it pursued economic policies more characteristic of center or even, in some cases, center-right European governments in the early 1980s.

The PSOE introduced its income policy of moderate wage increases in order to reduce real labor costs and aid the recovery of business profits. On the fiscal side, the party's policies sought to contain and reduce the public-sector deficit as a proportion of GNP. The Socialists' central macroeconomic focus in their first term was thus to stimulate investment by improving business profits, reducing financial costs, and granting more flexible tax allowances to new productive investment. The PSOE government combined these economic policies with attempts to reduce labor market rigidities, social security burdens, and losses of state-owned firms, and to restructure industry.

In some areas the Spanish economy responded well to these policies. Basic monetary aggregates slowed from 1983 to 1984. The public-sector deficit dropped from almost 6 percent of GNP in 1982, to 5.3 percent in 1983, and to 4.3 percent in 1984. Wages also moderated, reducing labor costs from 10 percent per unit in 1983 to 6 percent in 1984. The inflation rate (consumer price index) fell from 14 percent in 1982, to 12 percent in 1983, to 11 percent in 1984, lowering interest rates along with it. Conditions for investment also improved. Gross savings rose from 19 percent of GNP in 1982 to 21 percent in 1984. On the international economic front, Spain's balance of payments, assisted by an improved world economy, recorded a spectacular improvement, going from a $4.1 billion deficit in 1982 to a $2.1 billion surplus in

1984. An 8 percent growth in exports in 1983 and a 15 percent increase in 1984 facilitated an additional 2 percent growth in GNP in each of those years.

The economy, however, continued to perform poorly in three important areas: employment, domestic demand, and investment. Spain's official unemployment rate remained at 20 percent in 1985, affecting 7 percent of all heads of households and 50 percent of all young people under the age of 25. Structural constraints continued to impede domestic demand and investment to generate employment. Rises in real wages and social security contributions and market rigidities such as restrictions on dismissing employees distorted the equilibrium between demand for goods and services and demand for labor.

In the second half of the 1980s Spain was suitably rewarded for these first few painful years. Between 1986 and 1990 Spain's GDP grew faster than that of any other EC member state—nearly 4.5 percent per year, far outpacing the EC average of 3 percent per year. With this growth Spain's income per capita began to converge with that of its wealthier EC partners, rising from 73 percent of the EC average in 1986 to 80 percent in 1991—an increase from roughly $6,000 to $13,500. The stabilization policy succeeded as inflation fell from an average of 13 percent in the first half of the 1980s to under 7 percent in the second half and continued to decline to under 5 percent in early 1993. (See Table 4.)

Yet this rapid growth, combined with the strict monetary policy, led to an increasing trade and current account deficit. From just over $4 billion in 1984, the trade deficit soared to $29 billion in 1990. Receipts from tourism traditionally covered most of this deficit, but by 1991 they covered less than half of the trade deficit as revenues from tourism stagnated and Spaniards in-

TABLE 4. ECONOMIC INDICATORS, 1968–1993

INDICATOR	1968–1973	1974–1979	1980–1985	1986–1990	1991	1992
GDP (percent change)	6.7	2.2	1.4	4.5	2.4	1.2
Unemployment (percent)	2.7	5.3	16.4	18.6	16.3	18.2
Inflation (percent)	6.7	18.3	12.8	6.5	5.9	5.4

Sources: Loukas Tsoukalis, *The New European Economy* (Oxford: Oxford University Press, 1993), pp. 24–27; and "Survey on Spain," *Financial Times*, April 2, 1993.

creased their expenditures abroad. Consequently, Spain became more dependent on foreign investment, which more than made up for the lost tourism revenue; over $80 billion of foreign investment flowed into Spain between 1986 and 1991.[65] High interest rates, the economic advantages of access to the EC market, low wages and surplus skilled labor, and Spain's rapid economic growth enticed investors. However, a growing proportion of this money is composed of highly volatile portfolio investments. As discussed below, the collapse of the European Monetary System (EMS) and the recession of the early 1990s have increased volatility in this area as investors have sought safer havens. This loss of foreign investment further hindered economic growth.

Chapter 4

SPAIN IN THE 1990s

During the golden years of the 1980s the government of Felipe González achieved wide success in many of its endeavors. Spain moved from the periphery of Europe toward its core, and with advancements in economic and social welfare, Spain approached the standard of living of the most developed countries of Western Europe more rapidly than anyone had predicted a decade before. Many in Latin America and Eastern Europe viewed Spain as a model for successful transition from dictatorship to democracy. But success bred hubris, and the weakness of the opposition to the government brought complacency and even corruption into the upper ranks of the Socialist party.

THE PROBLEMS OF SUCCESS

The 1989 elections had seen a serious falloff in support for the PSOE, and at the beginning of the Socialists' third term as the governing party, a series of new problems surfaced, all of which worsened in the early 1990s. The PSOE's very success made criticism concerning its hegemonic role within the state inevitable.[66] Moreover, unresolved problems in the organization of the state complicated the PSOE's dual role as an administrator and as a political party within a democratically representative polity. First the opposition criticized the party for highhanded administration and material corruption, with accusations focusing on the family of then Deputy Prime Minister Alfonso Guerra. Second, as a political party, the PSOE faced the consequences of running the central government, which must deal with unassimilated nationalities (such as the Basques) and autonomous regional governments (such as Catalonia and Galicia) run by regional parties that could aspire to no more than minority-party status nationwide but were potentially key building blocks to any conservative opposition to the Socialists. These issues complicated center-periphery relations.

While economic prosperity continued and the PSOE enjoyed a clear majority in the Cortes, these difficulties remained muted and were almost never mentioned in discussions of the Spanish model. The opposition of large segments of the Basque population to the constitutional settlement of 1978, the continuation of Basque terrorism, and the failure to settle this issue remained troublesome indicators; also in this period, Spain lacked a conservative alternative, or even a viable democratic alternative, to the PSOE. The Socialists had so successfully preempted the conservatives' policies during the 1980s, in fact, as to undermine the possibility of an alternative government from the democratic right. And even if the conservative forces were to unite to win an election, the question remained as to whether they could hold together in government, particularly if the conservative coalition was based on disparate interests or a negotiated electoral pact incorporating regionally based parties, within and between which centrifugal pressures might reemerge like the tensions that destroyed the UCD. This vacuum in opposition clearly encouraged and aggravated the hegemonic tendencies within the

PSOE and complaints about its control of the state apparatus, as well as the potential for corruption.

ECONOMIC DIFFICULTIES

By 1992 Spain could no longer avoid the pains of a global recession and the strain of trying to fulfill the Maastricht criteria for economic and monetary union (EMU). Unemployment rose dramatically from 16 percent in 1991 to 22 percent in early 1993—by January 1993 more than three million Spaniards were unemployed. (Unemployment figures, however, are somewhat unreliable. Spain has a vigorous unofficial economy, and about one-third of those claiming unemployment are said to be employed part-time. There is probably substantial unreported income at the top of the economic spectrum, as well.) In addition, industrial production fell by 1 percent in 1992, and the performance in 1993 was little improved. Yet in the face of a declining economy, the country maintained high interest rates (13 percent in early 1993) to sustain the value of the peseta and to ensure a steady flow of foreign investment.

Spain's desire to be a senior partner in the European Community raises formidable economic challenges. This status will require membership in the EMU as set forth in the Maastricht Treaty. Prime Minister González staunchly believes that Spain must be part of the EC "core" that moves forward with EMU in 1997 or risk being relegated to the second of a two-tiered Community.

The Maastricht Treaty lays out strict criteria for entry into the EMU, including the following:

- Inflation over twelve months must not exceed by more than 1.5 percentage points the average rate among the three EC countries with the lowest inflation.

- Long-term nominal interest rates over twelve months must not exceed by more than two percentage points the average for the same three countries.

- The currency must remain in the narrow band of the exchange rate mechanism (ERM) for at least two years without a devaluation.

- The budget deficit should not exceed 3 percent of GDP.

- Total public debt should not exceed 60 percent of GDP.

Spain satisfies only the criterion concerning public debt, with a ratio at the end of 1992 of 46 percent of GDP. Concerning the other criteria, the rate of inflation remains about two percentage points above the target; the currency was devalued three times between the fall of 1992 and May 1993; Spain maintained a wide band within the ERM until the near collapse of the EMS in August 1993. (Since then all countries except Germany and the Netherlands have been granted wide bands indefinitely.) The budget deficit in 1992 exceeded 5 percent of GDP. To qualify for entry into EMU, Spain will have to undertake draconian measures to reduce government expenditures such as health spending, subsidies to state companies, restrictions on unemployment entitlements, and labor reforms.[67]

In April 1992 the government presented its economic agenda, entitled *Programa de Convergencia 1992–96*, which laid out its plans for attaining the Maastricht criteria. However, a year later it seemed doubtful that the government would be able to successfully implement this program as scheduled. The government has also had to contend with strong opposition to the plan, especially from the business community, which viewed it as a straitjacket on economic growth.

Nearly all of the economic targets provided in the plan have proven unobtainable in the short run and will remain difficult to obtain in the midterm. Whereas the convergence plan predicted GDP growth of 3 percent in 1992, in reality the figure barely surpassed 1 percent. The program forecast growth of fixed capital formation of 3.2 percent in 1992, but this figure actually fell by nearly 3 percent. Moreover, the government deficit was expected to decline to 4.4 percent of GDP in 1992, but official estimates show that the budget deficit exceeded 5 percent (unofficial estimations calculate the deficit at 8 percent of GDP). The program also anticipates that Spain's economy will grow at a rate 1 percent above the EC average and that over one million jobs will be created by 1996—both feats appear ever more in doubt.

The business community has little confidence in the convergence plan. Some 847 companies were forced to seek protection from their creditors in 1992, and business profits in general were down, affected by the high cost of borrowing made necessary by the government's efforts to defend the peseta within the ERM and attract capital to finance the budget deficit; furthermore, business is angered over government difficulties (for internal party reasons, among others) to liberalize labor legislation. There is also irritation within the old corporatist sector—especially where restrictive practices and cartel-like conditions prevail—at government efforts to increase competition. This involves both the professional sector (lawyers and architects, for example) and the service sectors, including telecommunications, real estate, and transport. The Tribunal de Defensa de la Competencia, under Miguel Angel Fernandez Ordoñez, has been investigating price fixing, monopoly practices, and reform of professional services under the terms of the convergence program. Many vested interests are unhappy as a result.

With the economic strains that achieving the Maastricht criteria will incur, the government faces a tough choice between short-term economic expansion and long-term convergence with the European Community. Prime Minister González has been outspoken in his conviction that Spain must be in the core of the EC as the Community progresses toward EMU. But the question remains whether the new government will remain committed to this painful course.

SOCIALIST FOREIGN AND DEFENSE POLICY

In Europe Felipe González has been a leading proponent of the European Union as envisioned by the Maastricht Treaty. Simultaneously Spanish foreign policy finally broke free of Francoist isolationism to play a leading role in both European and global affairs. Ironically, the great debate over Spain's participation in NATO occurred on the eve of changes in the international system so profound that the very existence of the Atlantic Alliance lost its rationale with the collapse and eventual disappearance of the Soviet Union. The end of the Cold War, however, very much helped defuse the contentious relationship with the United States, and despite the bitterness that had accumulated on both sides and Spain's opposition to the use of its facilities for "out-of-area" contingencies in the 1970s and 1980s, in 1990 Spain became a major staging area for the U.S. buildup in the Persian Gulf. Furthermore, against considerable internal opposition, Spain deployed naval forces of its own to operations in the Gulf, including one frigate and two corvettes. Cooperation with the United States was in remarkable contrast to the situation four years earlier when Spain denied U.S. jets fly-over rights during their bombing raid of Libya. During the Gulf war Spain allowed U.S. B-52 bombers to operate from Morón air station and even offered Spanish F-18s as escorts. The United States was also allowed to use Spanish military bases as major supply centers, and over eighty-five thousand U.S. troops transited through Spain.

Spain has also reemerged as an important actor in Latin America through active involvement in the promotion of peace in Nicaragua, El Salvador, and Guatemala. Spain has contributed 120 observers to the UN mission in El Salvador, as well as technical and financial support.[68] While Spanish and U.S. policy toward Central America often conflicted in the past, especially in the Reagan years, the two governments began working closely to promote peace in the region under President George Bush.[69] In its policy toward the Middle East, after decades of contention with the United States, Spain has also fallen more into line with its EC partners and the United States. The Socialist government established diplomatic relations with Israel in 1986, and Spain emerged as a prominent player in the Middle East with the convocation of the Arab-Israeli peace talks in Madrid in 1991. Furthermore, Spain has actively sought to re-create a community of Iberian-American nations through a series of conferences to promote better linkage among these states. Spain is the ninth-largest contributor to the UN budget and is a participant in a wide range of UN peacekeeping operations, including those in Bosnia, Angola, Namibia, and El Salvador.[70]

On January 17, 1986, in a momentous rupture with Francoist foreign policy, the Socialist government fulfilled its electoral promise of establishing diplomatic relations with Israel. Suffering from international isolation, Franco had sought close relations with any country prepared to assist Spain; with the Arab world willing to support Franco's regime, a special Spanish-Arab relationship had been established. Under Franco, Spain was a consistent and outspoken supporter of Palestinian self-determination, voting favorably for Arab causes in the UN General Assembly and supporting the Arab states in the 1973 Yom Kippur war against Israel. In exchange, Spain, which was almost completely dependent on imported energy to fulfill its needs, imported over 50 percent of its oil from Saudi Arabia and Iran, and during the oil crisis of 1973, it obtained preferential treatment from Arab oil suppliers. Fearing a deterioration of relations with the Arab world, Spain moved with extreme caution in recognizing Israel.

Spain was the final European state to establish diplomatic relations with Israel. The Socialist government's recognition of Israel culminated a relationship which began with Felipe González's visit to Israel in 1972 and continued in the relationship between the PSOE and the Israeli Labor party through the Socialist International. Benny Pollack argues that the anomaly of Spain as the only country in Europe not recognizing Israel became increasingly significant as it embarked on membership in the EC and NATO.[71] Thus, establishing relations with Israel marked a final transition from a traditional "Third Worldist" foreign policy toward alignment with the European Community and the Atlantic Alliance.[72]

While recognizing Israel, the government has worked to maintain good relations with the Arab states, especially in North Africa, and this approach made Madrid an acceptable venue for the opening of the Middle East peace talks in 1991.[73] Yet, as the Gulf war demonstrated, Spain's commitment to an Atlanticist-Europeanist foreign policy may at times conflict with its more even-handed approach to Middle East politics.

Within the European Community, Prime Minister González has been a leading proponent of a common foreign and security policy as envisioned in the 1991 Maastricht Treaty. González has stated that "the gulf crisis showed above all the need for a joint security policy as an indispensable element of a common foreign policy."[74] Spain supports the existing plan to create a Franco-German brigade that can be expanded to form the core of a European defense force.

Spain's defense industry has rapidly modernized over the past decade and in many respects is technologically competitive with those of its European partners. With a limited domestic market, Spain has become the eighth-leading exporter of arms. An important component of modernization has been coproduction with other European states, and the defense industry has become highly integrated with its EC partners through joint ventures, including the European Fighter Aircraft with Germany, Italy, and Great Britain; shipbuilding with Germany and the Netherlands; and the development of new missile technology with several NATO partners.

Although Spain is not a member of the military structure of NATO, it has, like France, negotiated a set of agreements outlining its military contribution to the Alliance. This contribution has been defined around six areas of coordination: defense of Spanish territory; air defense of Spanish territory and control of Spanish skies; control of the Strait of Gibraltar; naval and air operations for the defense of the eastern Atlantic; naval and air operations for the defense of the western Mediterranean; and Spanish territory as a transit and logistic support area for the Alliance.[75] Unlike France, though, Spain is represented in NATO's highest military authority, the Military Committee, and participates in many of the Alliance's military agencies.[76]

Spain's participation in UN peacekeeping forces in Namibia, Angola, Bosnia, and Central America marks a qualitative shift from rhetorical engagement to active participation in international activities. Spain's involvement in Bosnia is unique not only because of its size—over a thousand peacekeepers—but because Spain, like other troop contributors, will be paying the costs of the mission, which are estimated at 3 billion pesetas (approximately $25 million), and because its troops are "braced for casualties." This mission also demonstrates the change in the priorities of Spain's military from domestic politics to military professionalism. Indeed, while Spain is not a member of NATO's military structure, "some western diplomats believe that Spain . . . is testing the ground in Bosnia for what could be a readiness in Madrid to contribute forces to a future European rapid intervention brigade."[77] Thus, Spain's role in Bosnia marks a striking change from military isolationism to international activism.

Spain is, of course, a Mediterranean as well as an Atlantic power and has two vulnerable territorial enclaves in North Africa—Ceuta and Melilla. The Socialist government committed itself strongly to Spanish sovereignty for these enclaves while working diplomatically to encourage cooperation with Morocco. This effort succeeded in January 1991 when Spain and Morocco concluded the Treaty on Friendship and Cooperation.

Close proximity to North Africa and the enclaves of Ceuta and Melilla have made this region one of Spain's primary security concerns. This importance is reinforced by the fact that Spain imports more than 15 percent of its oil from North Africa, and Repsol, the state-controlled petroleum company, is actively involved in oil and gas exploration in the region. The focus on North Africa has heightened as nationalist and Islamic fundamentalist movements have gained strength across the region and as immigration to Spain has increased. With Spain's

involvement in the Gulf war sparking a wave of indigna-
tion in the Maghreb, Prime Minister González, the foreign minister, and a host of high-level officials visited
Maghreb capitals to prevent a collapse in relations. Recognizing the strong link between security and economics, Spain moved quickly to increase its aid and
investment in the region.

Madrid's long-standing worry about the consequences of instability in the Mediterranean and the
Maghreb has been manifested in its enthusiasm for the
idea of a permanent Conference on Security and Cooperation in the Mediterranean (CSCM), on the model of
the Conference on Security and Cooperation in Europe
(CSCE). Spain and Italy sponsored the proposal of a
CSCM, with the endorsement of France and Portugal, at
the September 1990 meeting of the CSCE. The proposal, however, gained little support from the United
States or other European states and appears to have
withered on the vine. Spain also sought to improve communication with the members of the Arab Union of the
Maghreb through the establishment of "5-plus-5" talks
between Spain, France, Italy, Portugal, and Malta, on
the one hand, and Mauritania, Morocco, Algeria, Tu-
nisia, and Libya on the other. These talks faltered as they
coincided with the rise of the war in Bosnia. However,
the door to improved communication and cooperation
with the Maghreb states has been opened.

The Socialist government also moved to improve
relations with Spain's immediate neighbors, France and
Portugal. The French rapproachement brought major
benefits for the anti-terrorism campaign; and regular
summits between Felipe González and the Portuguese
prime minister, Anibal Cavaco Silva, have helped to
diminish the ever-present Portuguese fear of Castilian
hegemony on the Iberian Peninsula.

THE OPPOSITION

The economic and political difficulties facing the PSOE by 1992 opened up opportunities on both the right and the left. The most formidable challenge came from the Partido Popular (PP), the successor of the Alianza Popular (AP), which Manuel Fraga Iribarne founded in 1979. Fraga had been a minister in Franco's regime, and public opinion considered the party reactionary and authoritarian. On a ten-point scale, with ten representing the extreme right and zero the extreme left, the AP scored 8.5 in a 1982 survey (while the average self-placement for the population was decidedly more center-left at 4.8).[78] To garner votes, the party formed electoral coalitions with a variety of center-right parties throughout the 1980s. Electoral support peaked in 1983 with 26 percent of the vote; once support began to decline in 1986, Fraga resigned as party leader. He was replaced in February 1987 by Antonio Hernandez Mancha, who proved too young and inexperienced to lead the party, which declined further in the polls. Fraga returned to take control of the party in January 1989 and changed its name to Partido Popular. But shortly before the elections he handed over control to José María Aznar, leader of the PP's new generation. In December 1989 the PP won an absolute majority in the Galician parliament, and Manuel Fraga became the regional president.

Throughout the first decade of Spain's democracy, the AP confronted a ceiling on its popular support because of its lingering connection to the Franco regime and the regional fragmentation of the right. With the replacement of Fraga by a new generation of leaders from the post-Franco era, the PP moved away from its roots and its reputation as a party of law and order. Shortly after taking control, Aznar was able to pension off most of the party "patriarchs" associated with the Franco era.

In the 1989 general elections the PP fared far better than expected and won 106 seats, one more than in 1986. Its success continued in 1990, when the party won four seats in elections in the Basque region, which is known for its anti-Franco sentiments. The PP progressed another step in the 1991 nationwide local elections, where it won 25 percent of the vote compared with 21 percent in the 1987 elections. It gained control of a number of large cities, including Madrid and the Socialist strongholds of Seville and Valencia, and won an absolute majority in twenty provincial capitals. The party's success was an important step in weakening the PSOE's mystique as the only party capable of governing Spain.

The PP has made an effort to seize the center of the political spectrum, which the PSOE so successfully penetrated in 1982. In the 1993 campaign the PP promised tax cuts, faster privatization, and cuts in interest rates. In this it gained strong support from the Spanish employers' organization, Confederación Española de Organizaciones Empresariales (CEOE), whose president, José María Cuevas, has been a vocal critic of the government. Such policies, of course, would be less responsive to the interests of foreign investors.

Convergencia i Unió (CiU), the Catalan nationalist party, won eighteen seats in the Cortes in the 1989 election. Catalonia is a formidable region: with a population of six million people, it accounts for 20 percent of Spain's economy and is home to nearly 30 percent of Spain's medium and large companies. The CiU is actually a coalition of smaller parties whose political philosophies are extremely heterogeneous, yet share the bond of Catalan nationalism. The party cannot be easily labeled as conservative or liberal, but overall it tends to be center-right. Its leader, Jordi Pujol, is also president of the Catalan regional government. Pujol leads a wing of the CiU that is strongly devoted to attaining maximum autonomy for Catalonia. His philosophical opponent is Miquel Roca, the parliamentary spokesman for the CiU in Madrid, who espouses a more moderate vision of Catalan nationalism and believes that Catalonia's future lies within Spain. While Pujol has tended to utilize antagonism with the central government in Madrid to rally political support, Roca has founded good relations with the PSOE, which has opened the door to the possibility of a CiU-PSOE de facto coalition.

Xavier Arzallus, leader of the Basque nationalist party, Partido Nacionalista Vasco (PNV), has retained a cautious relationship with the Socialists in the Basque regional government, where the two parties rule in coalition (the Socialists are the junior partner). Too much engagement in Madrid, however, risks alienating both conservative and nationalist forces at home. ETA, although severely weakened in recent years, retains the capacity to be a terrorist threat, and its political counterpart, Herri Batasuna, can count on as much as 18 percent of the vote in the Basque region. A considerable proportion of the Basque population remains committed to independence (see Table 5).

The far left party, Izquierda Unida (IU), which was founded in 1986, is composed of the former Spanish Communist party (PCE) and a number of left-wing splinter groups. Following its strong electoral performance in the 1977 elections, support for the far left dropped precipitously in the 1980s. This was the result of the philosophical struggle within the left and the emergence of a strong Socialist party. However, the IU, under the leadership of Julio Anguita, was able to resurge in the 1989 elections, capturing seventeen seats.

TABLE 5. PREFERENCES CONCERNING THE FORM OF THE STATE, BASQUE RESPONDENTS, 1977–1987

PREFERENCE	1977	1981	1982	1983	1987
Centralism	9%	4%	7%	2%	3%
Some autonomy	29	33	37	34	34
Much autonomy	32	13	18	24	20
Independence	24	21	17	26	31
Don't know	4	22	17	10	10
No answer	2	7	4	4	2

Reprinted from *Politics, Society, and Democracy: The Case of Spain*, Richard Gunther, ed., (1993) by permission of Westview Press, Boulder, Colorado

Support for the IU rose in 1993, owing to the defection of many traditional left-wing PSOE backers. It gained from the rise of "Euroskepticism" in Spain, having abstained in the parliamentary vote to ratify the Maastricht Treaty. The IU has also been a constant critic of the government's restrictive monetary policy. Prime Minister González and his more centrist colleagues were never enthusiastic about a coalition with the left, which would hamper its economic program, but this was always a preferred option for the left wing of the PSOE.

Sensing the Socialists' vulnerabilities, the main opposition party, the conservative PP, began to campaign in late autumn of 1992. In October 1992 the PSOE responded with an intensive campaign, ostensibly commemorating its ten years in power, that also allowed Felipe González to declare his intention to lead the party in the next general election.

However, 1992 proved to be a disappointing year for the Socialists. They had intended to celebrate it not only as the tenth anniversary of the PSOE's ascension to power, but as a year of affirmation of Spain's triumph over its turbulent past of civil strife and authoritarianism, and of its successful Europeanization, modernization, and consolidation of democracy. Furthermore, 1992 was the year of the Expo of Seville, commemorating the five-hundredth anniversary of the arrival of Christopher Columbus in the Americas, and of the Barcelona Olympic Games. But the economy deteriorated, and the party's association with corruption sullied its reputation. The economic downturn was sudden, with unemployment rising sharply, and the government forced to devalue the peseta twice within the EMS.

The corruption cases centered on a series of companies—Filesa, Malesa, and Time Export—found to have fabricated consulting reports in return for large fees from some of Spain's largest companies, including Banco Bilbao Vizcaya, Banco Central, and the engineering firm Asea Brown Boveri. These fees, in turn, were used to finance Socialist party expenses, including the rent for the party's headquarters. A PSOE-dominated investigating tribunal exonerated the party, but only after much delay and a deciding vote by the tribunal's PSOE-nominated chair. A subsequent judicial investigation has been continually undermined by the PSOE. The Socialists, it should be noted, are not alone in financing party expenses in this manner. Both the PP and the CiU Catalan coalition have been involved in similar scandals. But the Filesa affair seriously damaged the PSOE's reputation and served to revive interest in the case of Juan Guerra, which had forced the resignation of Deputy Prime Minister Alfonso Guerra in 1991.[79] Two years after the scandal broke, Juan Guerra was jailed for two years for tax evasion; he still faces further charges.

Other public relations disasters aggravated tensions within the party and between the party machine and the government. In broad terms this intraparty division is seen in Spain as being between the left and the so-called renovators, with the party machine controlled by the left-leaning Alfonso Guerra. Guerra used the tenth-anniversary campaign in 1992 to regain public attention. The prime minister himself and his finance minister, Carlos Solchaga, were in the midst of confronting Guerra's challenge when they had to divert their attention to the ERM crisis in the fall of 1992. The renovators are associated with Solchaga, Foreign Minister Javier Solana, and Narcis Serra, the former defense minister and Guerra's successor as deputy prime minister. The economic downturn in particular aggravated disputes over issues of central concern to the party and its union supporters, such as the economic reform program and a proposal to reform the strike laws.

Opinion polls in early June 1993 indicated that the Socialists could count on the support of only two of the seventeen autonomous regions—Andalusia and Extremadura, both regions where the government operates an unemployment scheme in which small-town Socialist mayors pay unemployed farm workers special benefits. Whether the PP could fully exploit the PSOE's difficulties with the electorate remained to be seen. But according to numerous opinion polls published during this period, the PSOE and PP were neck and neck. A large proportion of voters, however, remained undecided. It was these voters that the PSOE had to attract if it was to maintain power. Felipe González obviously hoped that he could come from behind and achieve a surprise victory like that of John Major in Great Britain in 1992. The government's mandate was officially scheduled to end in October 1993, but González called for the general election to be held on June 6, 1993. As it turned out, he was right to gamble.

Chapter 5

PROSPECTS FOR GONZÁLEZ'S FOURTH TERM

The European economic recession of the early 1990s, the dramatic consequences of the collapse of the Soviet Union and the communist regimes in Eastern Europe, the stalling of the high hopes for European integration, all had major impacts on Spain as it emerged from the 1993 electoral contest with a weakened central government and the serious and continuing problem of unemployment. The challenges ahead in the fourth term of Felipe González as prime minister will be formidable. Yet the success or failure of the minority Socialist government will determine the economic and political health of Spain as it prepares for the challenges of the twenty-first century.

THE 1993 GENERAL ELECTIONS

The outcome of the 1993 election places Spain in uncharted waters. The PSOE did not lose the election, as some had predicted, but it failed to obtain an overall majority and was unable to create a formal coalition. The Socialists were able to win 159 of the 350 seats in parliament with nearly 39 percent of the vote; this was above all else a personal victory for Felipe González (although this marked a loss of sixteen seats from the previous election). Having failed to win a majority of seats in the Cortes, the PSOE will be forced to govern through legislative cooperation with regional nationalist parties.

Lacking a parliamentary majority and with an array of controversial policies required, González could see his power in his fourth term quickly and easily unravel. The conservative Partido Popular and the communist-led coalition Izquierda Unida opposed González's nomination as prime minister. With the PSOE seventeen seats short of a parliamentary majority, the party relied upon the support of the center-right Catalan and Basque nationalist parties to attain an absolute majority in the vote to confirm him. González will, therefore, face the challenge of balancing the concerns of the left wing within his party and his more conservative coalition partners.

Eighteen years after the death of Franco, it appears the center-right has been accepted as a legitimate contender for political power and has freed itself from the shackles of its Francoist past. Thus, despite the fact that the PSOE will govern Spain, it was not the sole winner in the election. The PP raised its political status considerably, making the 1993 election the closest contest in post-Franco Spain. The PP gained thirty-four more seats than in 1989, winning 141 seats with nearly 35 percent of the vote, reducing the distance between the PSOE and itself from fourteen percentage points in 1989 to four percentage points in 1993. The PP also made important regional gains in the Canary Islands, Andalusia, the Basque Country, Catalonia, and Valencia. In absolute terms, both the PSOE and the PP increased the number of votes they received—the PP won 8.1 million votes, 2.8

million more than in 1989, while the PSOE won 9.1 million votes, an increase of 1 million.

One dramatic result of the 1993 elections was that the remnants of the UCD (renamed the Democratic and Social Center [CDS], in 1989), which governed Spain through the early and difficult period of transition to democracy, was unable to win even a single seat in parliament. With the PSOE moving progressively toward the center-left and the PP gaining legitimacy on the center-right, the CDS has been squeezed out of the political system. Although the regional nationalist parties remain important players, Spain appears to be settling into a two-party system.

The regional nationalist parties maintained a relatively stable level of support: the Catalan regional party, the CiU, won seventeen seats (compared to eighteen in 1989); the Basque PNV won five (the same as in 1989); and, somewhat surprisingly, the Canary Island coalition won four seats (compared to zero in 1989). Perhaps more important than the number of seats the CiU and PNV won is the fact that the Socialists will rely on them to govern the country. In exchange for their tacit support of the Socialist government, these parties will undoubtedly demand an increased transfer of responsibilities to their autonomous communities.

The left-wing IU increased its representation in the Cortes by one seat to eighteen, but this was disappointing, since less than a month before the election opinion polls had predicted the party could win up to twenty-seven seats. Because of the IU's anti-European platform and opposition to much of González's promarket economic agenda, the gap between the IU and the PSOE has widened, pushing the IU to the fringes of the political system.

The most immediate challenge to the new government is to surmount the economic crisis that has struck Spain and to prepare the country for entry into the EMU. González's primary task will be to develop a social pact between labor and business to implement tough economic policy changes. This will require deft negotiations to overcome the friction felt as the government attacks a large set of vested interests. Economic priorities, including wage restraint and liberalization of the labor markets, will require reconciling the demands of labor and employers, the interests of the probusiness nationalist parties (CiU and PNV), and the divisions within the Socialist party. Central to the refusal of either nationalist party to officially join a coalition with the PSOE were concerns that the PSOE-led government would not promote their economic concerns, but both parties left the door open to joining the government if appropriate policies were undertaken.

Divisions within the PSOE will pose a further challenge to the government in the coming years. Relations between Alfonso Guerra, who has long controlled the PSOE political machine and still commands much public support, and the government, led by his old cohort Felipe González, will be difficult. Guerra tends to support a more leftist agenda for the party than that favored by González and his team of promarket renovators. Setting aside their differences during the election campaign, González abruptly challenged the Guerristas after winning the election by proposing Carlos Solchaga, the former finance minister and an archenemy of Guerra, as the parliamentary leader and spokesman. In a hotly contested vote, the PSOE parliamentary group confirmed Solchaga by a margin of 87 to 66. This victory should further consolidate González's control over the party, but dissension within the PSOE remains high, along with the potential for internal conflict over key public policy questions.

After his eleven years in office, the political stamina of Felipe González will become increasingly important, and the PSOE will need to confront the question of a post-González era at some point between now and the official expiration of his term in 1997. During his third term, the press often criticized González for having lost interest in domestic politics as he concentrated on loftier issues, such as European integration. Now, with Spain suffering a stifling economic crisis, it will require all of González's considerable political prowess to overcome the obstacles that lie ahead. These economic choices not only are critical for Spain's well-being, but are central to González's mission of entrenching Spain in the core of the new Europe. González will face perhaps his toughest term in office as he seeks to mobilize support for austere policies while attacking numerous vested interests. Yet the opportunity is also at hand for González to complete the overhaul of the Spanish economy that he started in 1982.

THE ECONOMY

If Prime Minister González maintains his deep commitment to European integration, his government will finally have to confront structural rigidities that continue to plague the Spanish economy. With the Spanish economy suffering through a painful recession, the newly elected government will have to make forceful decisions in order to reignite the economy. The collapse of the EMS in August 1993 and the broadening of exchange-rate bands will allow the Spanish government greater flexibility over economic policy, especially interest rates, in the short run. Yet the pressure of attaining the Maastricht criteria for EMU continues. The EC remains committed to the existing timetable for establishing the EMU by 1997, and this will require the Spanish government to implement tough economic policies.

As discussed earlier, in the first half of the 1980s the Socialist government initiated an austere economic program of restructuring and stabilization that set the stage for an economic boom in the second half of the decade. However, confronting strong opposition from within the Socialist party and the unions, the government was unable to tackle a number of controversial issues such as rigidities in the labor market and lack of competition in the private sector. Spectacular economic growth in the 1980s masked these pervasive economic problems, which have come to the fore with the economy mired in recession in 1993. To reinvigorate the economy, many economists argue, the new government will have to move swiftly and forcefully to tackle remaining structural problems.

After leading all the economies of the Organization for Economic Cooperation and Development (OECD) from 1985 to 1990, the Spanish economy has fallen upon hard times, with a combination of international and domestic factors exposing its underlying weaknesses (see Table 6 for Key Economic indicators.). In the first quarter of 1993 GDP fell by 1.1 percent, following a 0.4 percent drop in the last quarter of 1992. Domestically, in the face of the economic slowdown the government has had to maintain a strict monetary policy and high interest rates to fight the inflationary pressure of its growing budget deficit. Following the Danish rejection of Maastricht, pressure on the peseta to devalue reinforced the need for high interest rates. As nervousness about the future of EMU spread across Europe, the peseta approached the lower bounds of its band in the ERM,

TABLE 6. THE SPANISH ECONOMY: KEY STATISTICS,
1991–1992

	1991	1992
Total GDP (billions of $)	527.1	575.7
Real GDP growth (percent)	2.4	1.2
GDP per capita ($)	13,509.0	14,723.0
Consumer prices (percent change)	5.9	5.4
Industrial production (percent change)	−0.9	−1.0
Unemployment (percent of labor force)	16.3	18.2
Public sector debt as percent of GDP	46.5	48.2
Money supply (M1) growth (annual percent)	16.8	5.5
Govt. bond yield (average percent)	11.85	11.96
Current account balance (billions of $)	−16.9	−24.6
Exports (billions of $)	55.2	59.2
Imports (billions of $)	86.9	96.4
Trade balance (billions of $)	−31.7	−37.2

MAIN TRADING PARTNERS (1991, PERCENT
OF EXPORTS AND IMPORTS)

	EXPORTS	IMPORTS
France	20.0	15.2
Germany	15.9	16.2
Italy	11.4	10.0
U.K.	7.7	7.5
U.S.	4.9	8.0
EC	70.9	59.9

"Survey of Spain," *Financial Times*, April 2, 1993, p. 2., and OECD, *Economic Surveys: Spain 1992–93* (Paris: Organization for Economic Cooperation and Development, 1993) forcing the government to sell reserves, maintain high interest rates, and suffer three devaluations within nine months.

A sharp fall in both domestic and foreign investment further hampered economic growth. Government investment fell sharply following the completion of major projects associated with the Barcelona Olympics and the Seville Expo. During the period 1984–1990, government investment rose by 15 percent per annum, but in 1991 it grew by only 9 percent, and in 1992 it rose by an anemic 2 percent. Simultaneously, business investment, which had doubled between 1985 and 1991, fell precipitously as interest rates rose, profits were squeezed, and bankruptcies spread. The international economic slowdown added to Spain's economic woes as foreign investment fell. After fueling the economy in the 1980s, private foreign investment dropped considerably from a high of $18.3 billion in 1990 to $15.6 billion in 1991 and $12 billion in 1992. In the near term the picture remains bleak as investment in capital goods fell 13 percent in the first quarter of 1993, after dropping 8 percent in the last quarter of 1992.[80]

The Spanish economy also suffered from declining competitiveness as the value of the peseta remained high (prior to its three devaluations) and wages rose rapidly. According to a survey of competitiveness by the Swiss-based World Economic Forum, Spain ranked near the bottom of the list of OECD members.[81] This decline, combined with the global recession, depressed exports.

Entry into the EC contributed significantly to economic growth in the mid-1980s, yet by 1991 the opening of the Spanish economy led to a dramatic rise in imports. Between 1988 and 1992 imports rose from $55.8 billion to $96.4 billion while exports rose only from $39.6 billion to $59.2 billion.[82] While imports rose by over 73 percent, exports increased only by 49 percent, creating an over-whelming trade deficit. The dramatic increase in imports endangered domestic producers and, combined with sluggish exports, sharply aggravated the external balance. This phenomenon was strengthened by the high value of the peseta, which at a time of growing consumption made imports that much less expensive. Eventually, the worsening external balance and the weakness of the economy became critical factors in forcing the devaluation of the peseta. Where EC membership was once viewed as a spark to economic growth, it now creates economic difficulties.[83]

While Spain must focus on domestic adjustments, in the short run its recovery is tied to the economic health of other EC members. As economist Juan Cuadrado and his colleagues point out, "the Spanish economy functions increasingly more in step with that of the EC, and the majority of the regions follow the fluctuations of the Spanish economy."[84] For example, 72 percent of Spain's exports are sold to EC members, and even following a 22 percent fall in the value of the peseta after three devaluations, export growth remains sluggish.

REGIONALISM

Although Spain, has been one of Europe's most unitary states since the eighteenth century, it is now rapidly becoming a quasi-federated, decentralized state. In a radical departure from Franco's suppression of Spain's nationalities, the 1978 Constitution "recognizes and guarantees the right of autonomy of the nationalities and regions," while reaffirming "the indissoluble unity of the Spanish nation, common indivisible fatherland of all Spaniards." In accordance with the 1978 Constitution, Spain is divided into seventeen regions, each endowed with its own president, parliament, and high court of justice (see Map 1). Furthermore, regional languages, including Euskera (Basque), Catalan, Galician, Valencian, and Majorcan are recognized as co-official languages. The Constitution opened the door to creating autonomous regions, but it also dictated that the process occur at varying speeds for each autonomous community.[85] The process began in earnest with the granting of autonomous status to two of Spain's "historic nationalities," the Basques and Catalonians, in 1979.[86] However, following the attempted coup in 1981, fear that this process would further alienate the military prompted a backlash against decentralization by Spain's two largest parties, the UCD and the PSOE. With the creation of the Law for the Harmonization of the Autonomy Process (LOAPA) in 1981, the process of decentralization was essentially stalled.

Yet by the summer of 1983 the formation of regional governments was completed as the autonomous community statutes for each had been approved and regional institutions were up and running. By the second half of the 1980s the process of regionalization regained vigor and has steadily progressed as the central government has devolved more and more responsibilities to the autonomous regions. This rebirth can be partially traced to the creation of the legislative pact in January 1985 between the Basque president, José Antonio Ardanza, and the Basque Socialist party. This agreement helped initiate the transfer of fourteen pending powers to the Basque government. Completion of the definitive financial arrangements for the period 1987–1991 also accelerated the assumption of increased powers and responsibilities by the regions. Decentralization is likely to continue as the influence of the Catalan, Basque, and other regional nationalist parties grows in national politics.

According to the 1978 Constitution, Spain's seventeen regions could attain their autonomous status through an accelerated process, described in article 151, or a slower, less-ambitious process, laid out in article 143. The accelerated approach was designed for those regions that had achieved or voted for a statute of autonomy during the Second Republic, most notably the Basque Country, Catalonia, and Galicia. The government created two distinct routes to autonomy to gain support for the Constitution and mitigate the continuing tension between the central government and the independence-minded Basque and Catalan regions. The government also hoped to prevent a Balkanization of the Spanish state through a nationwide movement toward autonomy.

Although there are two official routes to autonomy, the process of autonomization has progressed at radically different rates both between these categories and even within each one. There are four levels of autonomy among the regions: the Basques and Catalans have received the greatest autonomy; the Andalusians and Galicians are on the second tier; Valencia, Navarre and the Canaries are on the third tier; and the remaining regions are on the lowest tier. The Basque Country and Navarre, which experienced a high degree of autonomy dating back to the Fueros (historic rights) of the Middle Ages, were granted unique privileges including control over tax revenues.

The process of decentralization must conform to four basic principles. First, regional autonomy must not undermine the unity of Spain. Second, the process must not interfere with the central government's ability to maintain internal and external stability. Third, the process should enhance regional solidarity through a redistribution of wealth to the poorest regions. Fourth, the central government should ensure that regional governments have sufficient resources to finance the activities that have been transferred to them.

One of the most critical issues in the devolution of power is the ability of a region to finance its activities. The central government maintains control over most forms of direct taxation and distributes finances to the regions according to a complex set of calculations. The regions have little power to raise revenues directly, although this varies by region. Only the Basque Country and Navarre have direct control over the collection of revenues in their territories (but they must follow the basic tax guidelines set by the central government so as not to unfairly compete with other regions). In exchange, these territories contribute a fixed sum of their revenues to cover expenditures for activities undertaken by Madrid and for redistribution to the poorer regions. Other regions, Catalonia especially, have long pressed the central government for greater control over tax revenues raised within their territories.

Nationalist sentiment increased in the 1980s, especially in the Catalan and Basque regions. Polls taken on national and regional identification in 1984 and 1988, for example, found that in Catalonia the fraction who felt themselves to be more Spanish than Catalan had fallen from 11 percent to 8 percent, whereas those who felt themselves more Catalan than Spanish had risen from 22 percent to 25 percent. Those who felt themselves only Catalan had risen from 8 percent to 16 percent. In the Basque Country in 1986, 8 percent felt themselves only Spanish whereas those who defined themselves as only Basque reached 31 percent; those who felt themselves more Basque than Spanish reached 23 percent. By way of contrast, the same question to Andalusians found 57 percent in 1982 felt as much Spanish as Andalusian, and 66 percent felt this in 1986. Only 3 percent of Andalusians in each of these years felt more Andalusian than Spanish.[87]

Administratively, Spain is rapidly becoming a federated state as public expenditures and governance are shifted to the autonomous communities. While regional expenditures were nearly nonexistent in 1980, they had risen to 10 percent of GDP by 1991.[88] Moreover, the central government's share in public spending fell from 90 percent in 1980 to 67 percent in 1991. In contrast, spending by regional governments rose from nearly zero to almost 20 percent of public spending in 1991. Together, local authorities and regional governments account for one-third of public expenditures. Moreover, the regional governments play an increasingly important role in economic development. The regions' share in total general government capital expenditure is over 40 percent, and local spending brings the total to over 60 percent.[89] With the establishment of the autonomous communities and their new responsibilities, the number of civil servants based in the regions increased from 44,000 in 1982 to 565,000 in 1991.[90]

While some political elites feared that the creation of the autonomous communities would threaten Spain's new democracy, the well-known Spanish sociologist Victor Perez-Diaz argues that "on balance, the regional pacts have reinforced the degree of national integration."[91] An important factor has been the power of economics and industrial development. Businessmen and trade unions have been powerful centripetal forces, tending toward the integration of the national community. Catalans and Basques have occupied positions of leadership in the national employers and workers organizations; for example Carlos Ferrer, a Catalan, was leader of the Spanish employers association, the CEOE, and Nicolás Redondo, a Basque, leads the Socialist trade union, UGT. This phenomenon is visible today as the Catalan business association (El Club Financiero de Barcelona) has pressured the CiU to join a coalition with the PSOE in Madrid. At the same time, political scientist Robert Clark has argued in fact that a greater devolution of power is essential to economic development. He states, "If the experience of other West European and North American countries tells us anything, it is that [economic] transition must be accompanied by a loosening of the centralized and unitary controls."[92] Consequently, economics plays a balancing role of fostering decentralization, while reinforcing the cohesiveness of the Spanish state.

ECONOMIC DISPARITIES

Economic development among Spain's regions varies widely. The poorest region, Extremadura, has a GDP only 69 percent of the Spanish average, and Navarre, the wealthiest, has a GDP of 123 percent of the Spanish norm (see Table 7). The Socialist-led government, with a strong electoral base in many of Spain's poorer regions, has struggled to improve their economic conditions by channeling domestic and EC funds to them. While the central government has attempted to foster economic convergence, the results have been largely unsuccessful.[93] The gap between the richest and poorest has arguably decreased; unfortunately, the lowest regional GDPs have not risen toward the Spanish average; instead, the GDPs of some of the wealthiest regions have declined.

One of the tenets of decentralization policy is to maintain national solidarity through a redistribution of wealth to the poorer regions. After years of dormancy, regional economic development policy was revived in 1985, with the implementation of the Inter-territorial

TABLE 7. REGIONAL PER CAPITA INCOME AS PERCENTAGE
OF NATIONAL PER CAPITA INCOMES, 1990

REGION	PERCENTAGE OF NATIONAL PER CAPITA INCOME
Poor regions	
Extremadura	69
Andalusia	75
Galicia	76
Castilla–la Mancha	88
Rich regions	
Balearic Islands	121
Basque Country	112
Navarre	122
Madrid	121
Catalonia	112
Other	
Aragon	111
Asturias	93
Valencia	94
Cantabria	96
Canary Islands	101
Castilla y León	91
Murcia	98
La Rioja	107

Source: OECD, *OECD Economic Survey, Spain 1992–93* (Paris: OECD,
1993), p. 77.

Compensation Fund (ICF) and later with access to EC
regional development funds when Spain joined the
Community. Thus, in contrast to the Franco period,
regional development policy was not dominated by the
central government, but included new players, such as
the EC and the autonomous governments. As the autonomous communities gained greater responsibilities and
EC funding increases, these three parties were increas-

ingly obliged to work in cooperation to develop comprehensive development plans.

One explanation of the failure to equilibrate economic development concerns the approach that the government has taken toward improving living standards in
the poorer regions. According to Cuadrado and his colleagues, the government has focused too much on a
compensatory system aimed at raising disposable income
rather than creating "a favorable market environment"
that would attract investment and lay the foundation for
continued economic dynamism.[94] These critics argue
that while the current system relies largely on income
transfers through unemployment insurance and social
security payments, it should focus on improving the
underlying economic conditions by enhancing labor mo-
bility, moderating wages, expanding infrastructure, and
improving the education and training of the labor force.

The importance of a well-developed market structure for economic growth is evident through the flows of
industrial and foreign investment. The largest share of
productive investment tends to flow to well-developed
regions such as Catalonia and Madrid.[95] In 1987, for
example, Madrid received 32 percent of all foreign investment and Barcelona 33 percent.[96] Traditional economic determinants have been more powerful than government intervention. An exception is Andalusia, which
has been one of the poorest regions, but is the third-
largest recipient of foreign direct investment, averaging
9 percent of total foreign direct investment between 1986
and 1989. Andalusia also has been the largest recipient
of government assistance over the last decade, which has
contributed to the creation of a dynamic economy.[97]

Moreover, it is arguable that the current form of
regional aid has retarded economic development. First,
the compensatory nature of regional funds has protected

companies and families from increased competition, consequently slowing adjustment. Second, unemployment subsidies and social security transfers have helped prevent labor migration from poorer to richer areas and have prevented wage adjustment. Third, to avoid social conflict, the central and regional governments have allowed excessive social security fraud. According to Cuadrado and his colleagues, "Many families in those regions are still receiving the retirement pensions of long-dead relatives!"[98] Fourth, the location of state-owned industries in some regions has been detrimental because these industries pay higher wages than the private sector and tend to increase the average wage for the region. This inhibits further investment in labor-intensive industries.

One instrument the central government has created in order to lessen regional disparities in income is the Interterritorial Compensation Fund. Between 1984 and 1991 this fund disbursed 1.1 trillion pesetas (approximately $10 billion) to the autonomous communities. In comparison, funding from the European Community totaled about one-half this amount, 584 billion pesetas.[99] Unfortunately, the ICF has been largely unsuccessful in achieving its goal, primarily because the disbursement of funds has not followed strict economic guidelines and often has ended up in the hands of wealthier regional governments. The central government took steps in 1990, though, to remedy this problem and ensure that the ICF assisted only the poor regions.

FOREIGN AND DEFENSE POLICY

Responding to the dramatically changed strategic environment in Europe following the collapse of the Soviet Union, Spain adopted a new defense directive in 1992 to replace the directive of 1986.[100] The new policy guide-lines outlines the broad objectives of the military through the end of the decade, and declares that Spanish security is no longer confined strictly to Spanish territory and that the Western European Union is the key to the future defense of Europe and should represent the European pillar of NATO. It is a further demonstration of Spain's commitment to participating in a common European security policy as envisioned in the Maastricht Treaty.

The 1992 directive calls both for a restructuring of military forces and for further reductions in personnel. The plan calls for a rundown in personnel by the end of the decade to a force level of 170,000 men, of which 50 percent will be professionals (compared with the 1992 proportion of 30 percent). As mentioned earlier, mili-tary personnel has already been reduced dramatically, from 285,000 in 1988 to 217,000 in 1992, and the dura-tion of military conscription has been reduced. The plan foresees defense spending at a level of 2 percent of GDP, but with a growing budget deficit and economic diffi-culties, defense spending fell to 1.75 percent of GDP in 1991.

The new military directive also foresees the creation of a rapid action force, Fuerza de Accion Rapida (FAR) along the lines of the existing French Force d'Action Rapide. This force will be adapted to participate in crisis situations that require engagement by the WEU. The FAR should be operational by 1997, when Spain has completed the reorganization of its military structure, including a unification of its command, control, commu-nication, and intelligence (C^3I) structure.

Cooperation with France and Italy in the creation of the Hélios military satellite observation system marked an important step for Spain both to integrate its forces with its European neighbors and improve its C^3I structure. This was another decisive step in the acceptance and creation of a multilateral defense structure in Europe. The Hélios will open new doors to cooperation among these three and to their involvement in the WEU. In addition, the Hélios will offer improved coverage of the Mediterranean basin.

The 1993 elections in Spain focused primarily on domestic issues, but this did not mean that Spain had begun to turn inward again. In fact, Spain has finally and decisively abandoned its previous propensity toward isolationism as its domestic debates have become increasingly intertwined with its foreign relationships. In fact, Spain demonstrated its commitment to the world system by providing a large number of military personnel to the United Nations as well as by being the ninth-largest contributor to the UN budget. Furthermore, Spanish officials have noted that they would like to increase their contributions by earmarking funds specifically for peace-keeping operations in Latin America.

A broad-based national consensus has emerged on foreign policy, in contrast to the disputes of the early 1980s. Yet while Spain's security ties have become more multilateral and more West European–oriented, Spain has not broken its bilateral security relationship with the United States. And this stance is likely to remain unaltered through the 1990s.

Spain, however, continues to differentiate itself on important issues where it has historical or contemporary interests. For example, Spain's policy toward Cuba has been radically different from that of the United States ever since Franco refused to join the U.S.-led embargo against Castro beginning in the early 1960s. Over the years Cuba has been a source of continuous debate between Spain and the United States, and in 1992 the friction increased as a result of the U.S. attempt to apply its own laws outside its territorial borders through the Cuban Democracy Act. Washington's policy toward Cuba in fact remains largely immobilized while U.S. leaders continue to wait until Castro either dies, steps down, or is forced out. Spain, on the other hand, has always followed a policy of involvement, criticizing Cuba's human rights abuses, yet maintaining open channels of communication in an effort to bring about a democratic transformation.

A large degree of consensus in Spain also exists with regard to the regions perceived as security threats. Spain has long stressed the importance of the Mediterranean, citing risks from the south related to unequal economic divisions, immigration patterns, and growing Islamic fundamentalism in North Africa. During the 1990s the Maghreb and Mediterranean will become significantly important in terms of domestic policy and national security as Spain's leaders have to deal with issues such as migration from these regions.

Latin America likewise remains a priority. Indeed, Spain has been actively promoting peace and democracy in the region, especially in the Central American states of Nicaragua, El Salvador, and Guatemala. While Spanish policy ran counter to that of the Reagan administration, Spanish officials worked more closely with President Bush and would like to continue working closely with the Clinton administration.[101] Spain has been developing the concept of a community, or family, of American nations through a series of conferences involving the heads of state of Spain, Portugal, and the countries of Latin America (held in Mexico, Madrid, and Bahia).

Overall Spain's weight in Europe increased during the 1980s, with Spain acting as an important reference point for broadening the relationship between Europe and Latin America. Yet, events have occurred since 1989 that could not be foreseen. The worldwide recession, the debate in many European nations over the question of identity and their corresponding inward focus, and the dilemmas facing Eastern Europe after the dissolution of the Soviet Union all created dramatic changes in the European context. The end of the Cold War and the opening to the East have led to competition for Spain as many of the more developed Western European nations began to look toward Eastern and Central Europe, rather than southern Europe, for investment purposes. The profound changes in Europe, most particularly the re-unification of Germany, are bound in the medium term to affect Spain's position. If, in the longer term, this is accompanied by an expansion of the EC into Eastern and Central Europe, the balance of power within the EC will inevitably shift to the disadvantage of the southern members of the Community, thereby potentially diluting Spain's influence.

The primary dilemma the newly elected government will have to deal with is trying to articulate the desires and needs of the southern EC nations. Since the fall of communism and the reunification of Germany, the focus of the EC has shifted somewhat toward Eastern and Central Europe. These developments, especially the impact of the changes in Germany on the rest of the EC, has complicated the role of Spain (and other EC members) within the Community and will make it more difficult for Spain to reap the benefits of integration.

Overall, Spain's domestic achievements in the last decade have dramatically enhanced Spain's role on the international scene: as Spain modernized economically and politically and became "Europeanized" and more self-confident, it became a source of inspiration for other developing countries, particularly in terms of how it has dealt with the military and built a successful democracy.

Finally, as domestic and international policy issues become increasingly intertwined, the notion of social democracy and the definition of equity will pose acute dilemmas for a Socialist government seeking a balance between economic growth and social welfare. The new Spain is now a magnet for the rapidly growing and impoverished populations in North Africa. In the past the Pyrenees marked the border between the rich Europe and the poor Europe; now, as a result of Spain's economic and social convergence with the rest of Western Europe, the Mediterranean marks the divide between rich and poor. The question for Spain, as for all advanced societies, becomes: Can a welfare state be sustained without some limitations on entitlements, and without some exclusion and boundaries? Ironically, these problems are a measure of Spain's economic and social progress; they are the problems of wealth and not of poverty. In this, as in so many ways, the old Spain is gone, and a new Spain has emerged.

ECONOMIC AND POLITICAL AGENDA FOR THE 1990S

Spain's economic agenda for the 1990s is clearly laid out in its convergence program 1992–1996. The targets set in this program are extremely ambitious and are even more strict than those the EC laid out at Maastricht. The government expects to achieve these targets through stricter fiscal policy, structural reforms, and wage moderation. Attaining the Maastricht criteria depends upon the government's ability to control the budget deficit, inflation, and interest rates.

The three key goals of the convergence program are to reduce the government budget deficit to 1 percent of GDP, the current account deficit to 2.3 percent of GDP, and inflation to 3 percent by 1996. Attaining these objectives will be far more painful than expected in light of the difficulties the economy faced in 1992 and 1993. Given the prevailing economic environment, the underlying assumptions for this program were overly optimistic, particularly that of an annual growth rate of 3.5 percent and that of a decline in unemployment to 13.5 percent by 1996.

To attain the targets set out in the convergence program González will have to introduce policies that firmly demonstrate the government's commitment to reducing the budget deficit from its current 5 percent of GDP to 1 percent. As long as the government runs a large deficit, monetary policy must remain highly restrictive in order to repress inflation. This strict monetary policy, however, forces interest rates to remain high, consequently dampening economic growth. If the government can rein in the budget deficit, it will provide greater flexibility to monetary policy and foster a decline in interest rates.

Spain's large budget deficit is the result of the combined deficit of the central government and the regional governments. As the regions have gained greater autonomy and responsibility for a wider range of activities, their budgets have grown rapidly. The regional share of the overall budget deficit rose from 3 percent in 1982 to 29 percent in 1991. Yet there has been a lack of coordination in expenditures and employment between the regions and the center that must be remedied. In negotiating the new regional financial arrangements for the period 1992–1996, the regional governments agreed to cooperate with the central government in consolidating their budgets in order to fulfill the Maastricht criteria, but whether they adhere to this pledge remains to be seen. One problem lies in employment. As responsibilities devolve to the regions, they must create new government agencies and build a bureaucracy. However, reductions in the central government's bureaucracy have not occurred concomitantly with the transfer of responsibilities to the autonomous communities. Consequently, while the regional governments have expanded employment by more than 500,000 jobs between 1981 and 1992 (from 44,475 to 565,460), the central government reduced its payroll by just over 280,000 (from 1,181,820 to 900,576).[102]

Controlling inflation is another critical element in Spain's bid for membership in the EMU. In its convergence program, the government set a target for inflation at 3 percent per annum by 1996. In order to achieve this, the government must overcome several obstacles. First and foremost, as discussed above, it must reduce the budget deficit and government spending, which is largely responsible for inflationary pressure. Second, wage restraint must be achieved in both the public and the private sectors. In 1992 wages rose between 8 and 9 percent in the public sector and 7.5 percent in the private sector, far outpacing inflation.[103] This occurred at a time of growing unemployment and weakening economic activity. Third, the government must push ahead in deregulating the service sector, which is dominated by oligopolistic and monopolistic pricing. While prices in manufactured goods are quite stable, prices for services, which account for 25 percent of the consumer price index, continue to rise sharply. In 1992 alone the increase in service prices was 5 percent higher than that for nonfood goods.

While the government must give top priority to the creation of a stable macroeconomic environment, it must also confront the country's remaining structural rigidities. Most important is the continuing rigidity of the labor market. During the boom years, tremendous economic growth overshadowed the problems of the labor market. Spain led all OECD countries in job creation between 1985 and 1990, with more than two million new jobs (a more amazing feat given the rapid decline in employment in agriculture). However, as the economy slowed, unemployment rose rapidly in 1993 to 22 percent, with nearly three thousand jobs lost daily in the first few months of the year.[104] In 1992 alone over 400,000 jobs were lost.

While González was able to move his government toward the center in the 1980s and implemented a pragmatic, market-oriented economic program, he was unable to overcome resistance from within his party and from the unions to his effort to reform Spain's rigid labor market. The primary task is to abolish the old corporatist labor laws (*ordenzas laborales*) and provide greater flexibility to labor markets. To accomplish this, the government will have to address the concerns of both business and labor, by modifying the expensive and time-consuming procedures for laying off workers, reforming worker's rights to strike, controlling wages (for example, by abandoning indexation, as Italy has done), and building low- and middle-income housing to facilitate relocation of workers. The mettle of Gonzalez's government will be tested, though, as it faces ferocious labor union opposition to these policies.

At 22 percent in 1993, Spain's unemployment rate is the highest in Western Europe. This figure, though, is somewhat misleading since many Spaniards work in the country's underground economy. Moreover, because of lax oversight, many people are counted as unemployed and receive benefits even though they are not actively seeking work. Nevertheless, the unemployment rate could potentially worsen, as women's participation rate in the labor market increases. Spain's female participation rate is among the lowest in the OECD, but in the coming decade it should move toward the OECD average, adding several million potential new employees to the economy. The country is also facing a dramatic demographic phenomenon in the 1990s, with a large number of young people entering the educational system and the labor force at the same time as the percentage of older people increases.[105]

Modernizing and improving the educational system with an eye to the future needs of national competitiveness was a high priority of the Socialist government during the 1980s. Since 1982 the number of teachers in the public primary and secondary schools has increased by half, and the number of university students by three-quarters. Educational opportunities for women have also increased dramatically.[106] Yet while the improvements in education have been formidable, they are still insufficient for the demands of market conditions in the years to come, when Spain will lose its advantages of cheaper labor costs, and will need to compete in terms of educational and technical skills. The strains on the educational system caused by its large and growing student population have also created much dissension within the system towards the government. Following years of strong student support for the Socialists, the stridency of student hostility toward Felipe González was an important element in his decision to call an early election in 1993.[107]

One important requirement for increasing employment in Spain will be wage restraint. Between 1985 and 1990 increases in wages outpaced inflation and productivity, reducing Spain's international competitiveness.[108] Restraint will simultaneously enhance economic growth and reduce inflationary pressures.

Privatization and restructuring of state industries will also play a central role in Spain's economic agenda for the 1990s. As France has done, Spain will likely accelerate its privatization program as a way to restructure and modernize the economy and to cut the budget deficit through an increase in government revenues. But whereas France has a rich menu of public companies, Spain's menu is rather meager. According to one leading investment banking firm, Spain's most attractive companies include Repsol (energy and oil), Argentaria (banking), ENDESA (utilities), Ence (forest products), Telefonica (telecommunication), and Tabacalera (food and tobacco).[109] The privatization of these firms could provide several billion dollars to the government coffers. However, especially in a period of weak global economic growth, the government cannot move too quickly with privatization, or it risks overwhelming capital markets. This has occurred in Latin America, where market saturation has led to depressed values for companies being sold.

The ability of Spain to recover the spectacular growth rates of the late 1980s will depend upon the government's ability to shake free of the remnants of Franco's corporatist economy through restructuring and its ability to control government spending. But the task will be more difficult, since many of the economic benefits associated with accession to the EC have been consolidated. With the expiration of transition agreements and the implementation of the Single European Market (i.e., EC 1992), the Spanish economy is exposed to greater competition from EC members.

However, if the government can achieve the goals established in the convergence program, a renewed period of rapid growth is possible. If the government can control inflation, reform the labor market, and remove the remaining structural rigidities, Spain's competitive position will improve enormously. With lower inflation, lower interest rates, and higher worker productivity, the expectation is that foreign investment will again accelerate, profits will rise, and the external balance will improve.

Chapter 6

CONCLUSION

In the two decades since the death of Generalisimo Franco, Spain has experienced a spectacular transformation. Democracy is consolidated, and the country exudes a renewed self-confidence. The "Spanish model" has become an invaluable example of a peaceful and successful transition from an authoritarian to a democratic regime. Spain has simultaneously transformed itself from a highly centralized to a highly decentralized system of government, thereby mitigating many of the conflicts between the central government and the various nationalities incorporated within the Spanish state. Great progress has also been made in improving educational opportunities, social conditions, and the status of women and minorities. The professionalization of the army has led to its subordination to civilian control. Effective democratic leadership has emerged from an increasingly competitive representative political system. In these two decades Spain has transformed itself from an international pariah to a leading actor in the European and global arena. Notwithstanding the recession of the early 1990s, rapid economic growth has pushed Spain several notches up the ladder of industrial countries to the number eight spot among OECD members. Factoring in the underground economy, some economists argue that

Spain's economy is larger than Canada's, making Spain a candidate for the Group of 7 leading industrial nations.

Yet it is also clear that a new stage begins in 1993 and that Spain faces a number of formidable challenges in the years ahead. Former Education Minister José Maravall wrote in 1982 that Spanish democracy faced five problems: tension between the central state and peripheral nationalisms; a cynical view of politics and politicians; a serious economic crisis; social and economic inequality; and terrorism and violence.[110] During the 1980s the PSOE government made considerable advances toward solving each of these problems, but tensions remain.

As Spain moves toward the twenty-first century, the key question will be whether it can complete the economic transformation underway and join the upper echelon of European states. In 1993 Spain is suffering its worst recession since World War II, with unemployment at an all-time high. With a GNP per capita of only 80 percent of the Community average, Spain remains relegated to the "poor" tier of EC members, along with Greece, Ireland, and Portugal. While sectors within Spain are as modern and technologically advanced as any other in Europe, large regional and sectoral disparities inhibit the economy. Continuing the rapid progress toward economic convergence with the other EC members following admission to the Community in 1986 will likely prove more difficult in the years ahead. Having made a strong commitment to the creation of the European Union, Spain would have to rethink its policies within Europe if the Maastricht Treaty were to unravel.

The threat from terrorism also continues. While French cooperation since the late 1980s has assisted the government's battle against Basque terrorism, the threat has not been eradicated. ETA terrorism has been responsible for 750 deaths over the past twenty-five years. Considerable progress has been made in controlling terrorism, and attitudes in the Basque Country toward ETA terrorists are slowly changing. Yet dozens of people continue to be murdered annually in terrorist attacks. After a lull in 1992 and 1993, ETA terrorists reasserted themselves by killing seven people in Madrid on June 21, 1993, when two car bombs exploded. As the Basque government increases its cooperation with the central government, Basque terrorists may be tempted to renew terrorist campaigns. Overall, however, Basque terrorism no longer poses a serious threat to Spain's stability, and terrorists are becoming increasingly isolated from a population that no longer supports their cause.

Problems with regional autonomy remain and tension between the regions and the central government persist. Prime Minister González has committed himself to furthering progress on regionalization; he has named Jeronimo Saavedra, the former president of the Canary Islands, to oversee the Ministry of Public Administration, which is responsible for regional policy. The Basque and Catalan regional parties will play a more important role in the national political process after the 1993 elections, but they will demand an acceleration of the devolution of power to the regional authorities. The Constitution is extremely vague regarding the specific powers that must be transferred, and an extended tug-of-war between the central government and the regions is likely. Social and economic inequality also remains high, and to a large extent economic growth over the last decade has aggravated the inequality between rich and poor Spain. In the medium term, without a resolution to this problem, tension within the Spanish state will continue.

Over the next decade a growing tide of immigration will challenge Spain, a country accustomed to sending its people abroad. Traditionally, migrants have used Spain as a transit route to the wealthier countries to the north, but more and more, immigrants from North Africa are settling in Spain. As demographic pressures increase in the Maghreb, this trend is likely to increase. Spanish society may be no more ready to accept this change than other European countries are. The emergence of right-wing, xenophobic extremism from some quarters is not impossible.

Last, with nearly every political party implicated in corruption and scandal, the general public remains highly cynical about politicians and politics. Increased transparency in party funding is needed to provide greater accountability. Corruption and scandal emerged as critical issues in the 1993 campaign, and Spain should react quickly to this problem in order to avoid the type of political disgrace and resentment toward a corrupt political class that has emerged in Italy.

It is a measure of Spain's remarkable progress since 1975 that many of the problems that the minority Socialist government faces in the 1990s are also Europe's problems. And in a wider context, even the challenges to the Spanish democratic model, especially the complex emotional, historical, and cultural question of creating a multinational state, look exemplary against the background of the ongoing bloodbath in the Balkans. The presence of Spanish military units in Bosnia and Herzegovina, where they are participating in the UN peacekeeping force, is in many ways emblematic of the new Spain. Here is the reformed Spanish military, fully part of the international system, seeking to contain a conflagration which in its viciousness and international implications is not unlike the civil breakdown in Spain's recent past—a past that Spain has triumphantly escaped.

FURTHER READING

Christopher Abel and Nissa Torrents, eds., *Spain: Conditional Democracy* (New York: St. Martin's Press, 1984).

Oscar Alzaga, *Comentario sistemático a la constitución Española de 1978* (Madrid: Ediciones del Foro, 1978).

Charles W. Anderson, *The Political Economy of Modern Spain: Policy Making in an Authoritarian System* (Madison: University of Wisconsin Press, 1970).

David S. Bell, ed., *Democratic Politics in Spain: Spanish Politics After Franco* (New York: St. Martin's Press, 1983).

Hans Binnendijk, ed., *Authoritarian Regimes in Transition* (Washington, D.C.: Center for the Study of Foreign Affairs, Foreign Service Institute, U.S. Department of State, 1987).

Christopher Bliss and Jorge Braga de Macedo, eds., *Unity with Diversity in the European Economy: The Community's Southern Frontier* (Cambridge, England: Cambridge University Press, 1990).

Andrea Bonime-Blanc, *Spain's Transition to Democracy: the Politics of Constitution Making* (Boulder, Colo.: Westview Press, 1987).

Michael Buse, *La Nueva Democracia Española: Sistema de partidos y Orientación del Voto (1970–1983)* (Madrid: Unión Editorial, 1984).

Raymond Carr, *Modern Spain, 1875–1980* (Oxford: Oxford University Press, 1980).

Raymond Carr and Juan Pablo Fusi, *Spain: Dictatorship to Democracy* (London: Allen and Unwin, 1979).

Robert P. Clark and Michael H. Haltzel, eds., *Spain in the 1980s: The Democratic Transition and a New International Role* (Cambridge, Mass.: Ballinger Publishing Company, 1987).

Robert P. Clark, *The Basques: The Franco Years and Beyond* (Reno, Nev.: University of Nevada Press, 1979).

Congressional Research Service, *A Report on West European Communist Parties* (Washington, D.C.: Congressional Research Service, 1977).

Peter J. Donaghy and Michael T. Newton, *Spain: A Guide to Political and Economic Institutions* (Cambridge: Cambridge University Press, 1987).

Gerald A. Dorfman and Peter J. Duignan, eds., *Politics in Western Europe* (Palo Alto, Calif.: Hoover Institute Press, 1991).

Samuel D. Eaton, *The Forces of Freedom in Spain, 1974–1979: A Personal Account* (Palo Alto, Calif.: Hoover Institute Press, 1981).

The Economist, "After the Fiesta: A Survey of Spain," April 25th, 1992.

Richard S. Fischer, "The Spanish Left: Resurgence After Four Decades of Franco," Western Societies Program, Occasional Papers, no. 11, (Ithaca, N.Y.: Cornell University, 1978).

Robert M. Fishman, "The Labor Movement in Spain, from Authoritarianism to Democracy," *Comparative Politics* vol. 14 (April 1982), pp. 281–305.

Juan Pablo Fusi, *Franco: A Biography* (New York: Harper & Row, 1987).

Antonio Garriques y Díaz-Cañabote, Rafael Luis Bardojí, et al, *España dentro de la Alianza Atlantica*, (Madrid: Instituto de Cuestiones Internacionales, 1988).

Charles F. Gallagher, *Culture and Education in Spain. Part VI: Franco's Spain (1936–1975)*, American Universities Field Staff Reports no. 24, 1979.

Richard Gillespie, *The Spanish Socialist Party: A History of Factionalism* (Oxford: Oxford University Press, 1989).

———"Spain's Referendum on NATO," *Western European Politics*, vol. 9, no. 4 (October 1986), 238–44.

David Gilmour, *The Transformation of Spain: From Franco to the Constitutional Monarchy* (London: Quartet Books, 1985).

Alberto Giovannini, ed., *Finance and Development: Issues and Experience* (Cambridge: Cambridge University Press, 1993).

George E. Glos, "The New Spanish Constitution: Comments and Full Text," *Hastings Constitutional Law Quarterly* vol. 7 (Fall 1979), pp. 47–128.

Robert Graham, *Spain: A Nation Comes of Age* (New York: St. Martin's Press, 1984).

Richard F. Grimmett, *U.S.-Spanish Bases Agreement* (Washington, D.C.: Congressional Research Service, Library of Congress, 1988).

Alfonso Guerra and Jose Felix Tezanos, eds., *La Decada del Cambio: Diez Años de Gobierno Socialista (1982-1992)* (Madrid: Editorial Sistema, 1993).

Richard Gunther, Giacomo Sani, and Goldie Shabad, *Spain after Franco: The Making of a Competitive Party System* (Berkeley: University of California Press, 1986).

Richard Gunther, ed., *Politics, Society, and Democracy: The Case of Spain* (Boulder, Colo.: Westview Press, 1993).

———"Spain and Portugal," in Gerald A. Dorfman and Peter J. Duignan eds., *Politics in Western Europe* (Palo Alto, Calif.: Hoover Institution Press, 1991), pp. 214-64.

Joseph Harrison, *The Spanish Economy in the Twentieth Century* (New York: St. Martin's Press, 1985).

John H. Herz, ed., *From Dictatorship to Democracy: Coping with the Legacies of Authoritarianism and Totalitarianism* (Westport, Conn.: Greenwood Press, 1982).

John Higley and Richard Gunther, eds., *Elites and Democratic Consolidation in Latin America and Southern Europe* (Cambridge: Cambridge University Press, 1992).

International Institute for Strategic Studies, *The Military Balance* (London: Brassey's, 1992).

Lawrence S. Kaplan, Robert W. Clawson, and Raimondo Luraghi, eds., *NATO and the Mediterranean* (Wilmington, Delaware: Scholarly Resources, 1985).

Beate Kohler, *Political Forces in Spain, Greece and Portugal* (London: Butterworth, 1982).

Thomas D. Lancaster and Gary Prevost, eds., *Politics and Change in Spain* (New York: Praeger, 1985).

Joyce Lasky Shub and Raymond Carr, eds., *Spain: Studies in Political Security* (New York: Praeger, 1985).

Ian O. Lesser, *Mediterranean Security: New Perspectives and Implications for U.S. Policy* (Santa Monica, Calif.: Rand, 1992).

Juan Linz, "Europe's Southern Frontier: Evolving Towards What?" *Daedalus*, Winter 1979, pp. 175-209.

Jonathan Marcus, "The Triumph of Spanish Socialism: The 1982 Elections," *Western European Politics*, vol. 6, no. 3 (July 1983), pp. 281-86.

José Maria Maravall, *Dictatorship and Political Dissent* (London: Tavistock, 1978).

———"Remarques sur le mouvement ouvrier dans la transition à la démocratie en Espagne," *Pouvoirs*, no. 8 (1979).

———"Political Cleavages in Spain and the 1979 General Election," *Government and Opposition*, vol. 14 (Summer 1979), 299-317.

———*The Transition to Democracy in Spain* (New York: St. Martin's Press, 1982).

Kenneth Maxwell, ed., *The Press and the Rebirth of Iberian Democracy* (Westport, Conn., Greenwood Press, 1983).

———ed., *Spanish Foreign and Defense Policy* (Boulder, Colo.: Westview Press, 1991).

———"Spain and Portugal and the Alliance: Prospects and Difficulties," *American Foreign Policy Newsletter* (April 1986).

———"Spain's Transition to Democracy: A Model for Eastern Europe?" in Nils H. Wessell, *The New Europe: Revolution in East-West Relations* (New York: The Academy of Political Science, 1991), pp. 35–49.

———"The Emergence of Democracy in Spain and Portugal," *Orbis*, vol. 27, no. 1 (Spring 1983), pp. 151–84.

Peter McDonough, Antonio López Pina, and Samuel H. Barnes, "The Spanish Public in Political Transition," *British Journal of Political Science*, vol. 11 (1981), pp. 49–79.

Kenneth Medhurst, "Spain's Evolutionary Pathway from Dictatorship to Democracy," *West European Politics*, vol. 7, no. 2 (April 1984), pp. 30–50.

Tomás Mestre Vives, *La Politica Iberoamericana del Gobierno Socialista Español* (Madrid: Instituto de Cuestiones Internacionales, 1985).

Edward Moxon-Browne, *Political Change in Spain* (London: Routledge Press, 1989).

Eusebio Mujal Leon, *Communism and Political Change in Spain* (Bloomington: Indiana University Press, 1983).

———"Decline and Fall of Spanish Communism," *Problems of Communism*, vol. 35, March/April 1986, pp. 1–27.

———"The Left and the Catholic Question in Spain," *Western European Politics*, April 1982, pp. 32–54.

Elizabeth Nash, "The Spanish Socialist Party Since Franco," in David S. Bell, ed., *Democratic Politics in Spain: Spanish Politics After Franco* (New York: St. Martin's Press, 1983), pp. 29–62.

John Naylor, "Spain, Portugal and the EEC: A Troublesome Enlargement," *Bank of London and South American Review* (August 1981).

C. Moya, *El poder económico en España* (Madrid: Túcar, 1975).

Guillermo O'Donnell, Phillipe C. Schmitter, and Laurence Whitehead, *Transitions from Authoritarian Rule* (Baltimore, Md.: Johns Hopkins University Press, 1986).

Organization for Economic Cooperation and Development, *Economic Surveys: Spain 1992–93* (Paris: OECD, 1993).

Francisco Oriza, *Juventud Española 1984* (Madrid: Ediciones S.M., 1985).

Stanley G. Payne, *Basque Nationalism* (Reno, Nev.: University of Nevada Press, 1975).

——*Franco* (Madison, Wis.: University of Wisconsin Press, 1991).

——*Franco: El Perfil de la Historia* (Madrid: Espasa-Calpe, 1992).

——ed., *The Politics of Democratic Spain* (Chicago: Chicago Council on Foreign Relations, 1986).

——"Catalan and Basque Nationalism," *Contemporary History*, vol. 6, no. 1, 1979.

Howard Penniman and Eusebio Mujal-León, *Spain at the Polls* [1977, 1979, and 1982] (Durham, N.C.: Duke University Press).

Victor M. Perez-Diaz, *The Return of Civil Society: The Emergence of Democratic Spain* (Cambridge, Mass.: Harvard University Press, 1993).

Rafael López Pintor, *La Opinión Publica Española: del Franquismo a la Democracia* (Madrid: Centro de Investigaciones Sociales, 1982).

Carlos Robles Piquer, "Spain in NATO: An Unusual Kind of Participation," *Atlantic Community Quarterly*, vol. 24, no. 4 (Winter 1986/87).

Benny Pollack, *The Paradox of Spanish Foreign Policy* (New York: St. Martin's Press, 1987).

Paul Preston, ed., *Spain in Crisis* (New York: Harper & Row, 1976).

——*The Triumph of Democracy in Spain* (New York: Methuen, 1986).

——*Franco: A Biography* (New York: Harper Collins, 1993).

Paul Preston and Dennis Smyth, *Spain, the EEC, and NATO*, Chatham House Paper no. 22 (London: Routledge, 1984).

Antonio Ramos Gascon, ed., *España Hoy* (Madrid: Ediciones Catedra, 1991).

Keith G. Salmon, *The Modern Spanish Economy* (London: Pinter, 1991).

Antonio Sánchez-Gijón, *El gasto de defensa y el gasto militar en España, 1975–1982* (Madrid: Instituto de Cuestiones Internacionales, 1982).

Donald Share, *Dilemmas of Social Democracy: The Spanish Socialist Workers Party in the 1980s* (New York: Greenwood Press, 1989).

Stockholm International Peace Research Institute (SIPRI) Yearbook, *World Armaments and Disarmaments* (Oxford: Oxford University Press, 1992).

Eric Solsten and Sandra W. Meditz, eds., *Spain: A Country Study* (Washington, D.C.: Library of Congress, 1990).

Jordi Solé Tura, *Nacionalidades y Nacionalismos en España* (Madrid: Alianza Editorial, 1985).

Claire Spencer, "The Maghreb in the 1990s," *Adelphi Papers*, no. 274, (London: Brassey's, 1993).

Stephen Szabo, ed., *The Successor Generation* (London: Butterworth, 1983).

Alfred Tovias, *Foreign Economic Relations of the European Community: The Impact of Spain and Portugal* (Boulder, Colo.: Lynne Rienner Publishers, 1990).

Gregory F. Treverton, "Spain: Domestic Politics and Security Policy," *Adelphi Papers*, no. 204 (London: Brassey's, 1986).

Loukas Tsoukalis, *The European Community and Its Mediterranean Enlargement* (London: Allen and Unwin, 1981).

———*The New European Economy* (Oxford: Oxford University Press, 1993).

Javier Tusell and Justino Sinova, eds., *La Decada Socialista: El Ocaso de Felipe González* (Madrid: Editorial Espasa-Calpe, 1992).

José Vidal-Beneyto, ed., *España a debate* (Madrid: Editorial Tecnos, 1991).

José Viñals, ed., *La Economía Española ante el Mercado Unico Europeo* (Madrid: Alianza Editorial, 1992).

———et al., "Spain and the 'EC cum 1992' Shock," in Christopher Bliss and Jorge Braga de Macedo, *Unity with Diversity in the European Economy: The Community's Southern Frontier* (Cambridge: Cambridge University Press, 1990), pp. 145–234.

Howard J. Wiarda, *The Transition to Democracy in Spain and Portugal* (Washington, D.C.: American Enterprise Institute, 1989).

———ed., *The Iberian–Latin American Connection: Implications for U.S. Foreign Policy* (Boulder, Colo.: Westview Press, 1986).

Colin Williams, ed., *National Separatism* (Vancouver: University of British Columbia Press, 1982).

Alison Wright, *The Spanish Economy, 1959–1976* (London: Macmillan, 1977).

NOTES

1. As late as 1989, Howard Wiarda stated: "I remain uncertain how deeply the democratic ethos has been internalized within the Spanish and Portuguese political culture, whether democracy is viable there, how strongly it is wanted, and whether it will last." See Howard J. Wiarda, *The Transition to Democracy in Spain and Portugal* (Washington, D.C.: American Enterprise Institute, 1989), p. x.
2. Remarks at conference, "Spain on the Eve of the General Elections," Council on Foreign Relations, New York, New York, May 3, 1993.
3. For a good general overview of Franco and the transition in Spain, see Raymond Carr and Juan Pablo Fusi, *Spain: Dictatorship to Democracy* (London: Allen and Unwin, 1979). See also Juan Pablo Fusi, *Franco: A Biography* (New York: Harper & Row, 1987), Stanley G. Payne, *Franco: El Perfil de Historia* (Madrid: Espasa-Calpe, 1992), and Paul Preston, *Franco: A Biography* (New York: Harper Collins, 1993).
4. See Eric N. Baklanoff, "The Economic Transformation of Spain: Systemic Change and Accelerated Growth, 1959–73," *World Development* vol. 4, no. 9 (1976), pp. 749–59.
5. See the wide-ranging discussion by Juan Linz, "Europe's Southern Frontier: Evolving towards What?" in *Daedalus*, vol. 108, no. 1 (Winter 1979), pp. 175–209, and Victor M. Perez-Diaz, *The Return of Civil Society: The Emergence of Democratic Spain* (Cambridge, Mass.: Harvard University Press, 1993). Juan Linz's extensive contributions to the study of contemporary Spain are discussed in the recent festschrift by Richard Gunther, ed., *Politics, Society and Democracy: The Case of Spain* (Boulder, Colo.: Westview Press, 1993).
6. The dates of the three successive development plans were 1964–67, 1968–71, and 1972–75. See Charles W. Anderson,

The Political Economy of Modern Spain: Policy Making in an Authoritarian System (Madison: University of Wisconsin Press, 1970). See also Alison Wright, *The Spanish Economy 1959–1976* (London: Macmillan, 1977); and Jurgen Donges, "From Autarchic Towards a Cautiously Outward-Looking Industrialization Policy: The Case of Spain," *Weltwirtschaftliches Archiv*, vol. 107, no. 1 (1971), pp. 48–50.

7. The Vatican's recognition of Franco's government in the Concordat of August 1953—signed shortly before the defense agreement with the United States—furnished his regime increased domestic and international respectability. The concordat declared Spain a Catholic confessional state and provided wide-ranging economic and legal privileges to the church. The Pact of Madrid, signed September 20, 1953, contained three executive agreements that pledged the United States to furnish economic and military aid to Spain in exchange for the right to construct and utilize air and naval bases on Spanish territory. Between 1954 and 1982 the United States provided Spain military aid of over $1.7 billion in grants and loans. See Eric Solsten and Sandra Meditz, eds., *Spain: A Country Study* (Washington, D.C.: Library of Congress, 1990), p. 321.

8. For a summary of the statistical data, see Linz, "Europe's Southern Frontier."

9. For a good discussion, see Loukas Tsoukalis, *The European Community and Its Mediterranean Enlargement* (London: Allen and Unwin, 1981).

10. On the labor movement in Spain, see José Maria Maravall, "Remarques sur le mouvement ouvrier dans la transition à la démocratie en Espagne," *Pouvoirs*, no. 8 (1979); and his *Dictatorship and Political Dissent* (London: Tavistock, 1978). See also Robert M. Fishman, "The Labor Movement in Spain, from Authoritarianism to Democracy," *Comparative Politics* (April 1982), pp. 281–305; and Joseph W. Foweraker, "The Role of Labor Organizations in the Transition to Democracy in Spain," in Robert Clark and Michael Haltzel, eds., *Spain in the 1980s* (Cambridge, Mass.: Ballinger, 1987), pp. 97–122.

11. See José Maria Maravall, "Political Cleavages in Spain and the 1979 General Election," *Government and Opposition*, vol. 14 (Summer 1979), pp. 299–317; and Linz, "Europe's Southern Frontier," p. 180.

12. On educational change in Spain, see Charles F. Gallagher, *Culture and Education in Spain. Part VI: Franco's Spain (1936–1975)*, American Universities Field Staff Reports, no. 24, 1979.

13. For a good overview of the economic impact of recession on Spain and Portugal, see John Naylor, "Spain, Portugal and the

EEC: A Troublesome Enlargement," *Bank of London and South American Review* (August 1981), pp. 122–30.

14. Samuel D. Eaton, *The Forces of Freedom in Spain, 1974–1979: A Personal Account* (Palo Alto, Calif.: Hoover Institute Press, 1981).

15. See Vernon A. Walters, *Silent Missions* (Garden City, N.Y.: Doubleday & Co., 1978), pp. 551–557.

16. For example, Barbara Probst Solomon, a very well-informed observer of Spain, wrote in the preface to her translation and adaptation of Julian Agirre's book, *Operation Orgo: The Execution of Admiral Carrero Blanco* (New York: Quadrangle, 1975), p. xi, that "one thing is certain: the careful success [sic] to power Franco had firmly mapped out has been shaken [by Carrero Blanco's assasination]. Spain is on the verge of political chaos."

17. During this period, the creation of a free press played a critical role. With a lack of democratic institutions, the newly established media, such as *Cambio 16* and *El Pais*, offered a means for open political debate and expression that to a certain extent substituted for a functioning, democratic parliament. See Kenneth Maxwell, ed., *The Press and the Rebirth of Iberian Democracy* (Westport, Conn.: Greenwood Press, 1983); and Antonio Sánchez-Gijón, "The Spanish Press in the Transition Period," in Clark and Haltzel, *Spain in the 1980s*.

18. This occurred over the period 1978–1979. The key events were as follows: First, in December 1978 the constitution was approved in parliament and then approved in a popular referendum. Second, in March 1979, the first general election took place under the new Constitution. Finally, in April 1979, the first free local elections took place under the new system of government. The process of pact making occurred on both sides in Spain. The key events were the establishment in March 1976 of a united coalition of all the anti-Franco forces in the Coordinación Democrática (which succeeded the Junta Democrática set up in Paris in 1974); and the October 1977 formulation of the Moncloa Pact, based on an agreement among the three largest national parties at the time (the UCD, the PSOE, and the PCE) regarding measures aimed at correcting short-term disequilibrium in the economy and regarding the reform of monetary and financial systems. However, until late 1977, the opposition forces had hoped for a "democratic rupture," but they were neutralized by groups within the regime. The political initiative in fact was held throughout this period by Prime Minister Suárez and the so-called civilized right. See David Gilmour, *The Transformation of Spain: From Franco to the Constitutional*

Monarchy (London: Quartet Books, 1985); and Robert Graham, *Spain: A Nation Comes of Age* (New York: St. Martin's Press, 1984).

19. See Elizabeth Nash, "The Spanish Socialist Party since Franco," in David Bell, ed., *Democratic Politics in Spain: Spanish Politics after Franco* (New York: St. Martin's Press, 1983), pp. 29–62; and Richard Gunther, Giacomo Sani, and Goldie Shabad, *Spain after Franco: The Making of a Competitive Party System* (Berkeley: University of California Press, 1986). See also Richard Gillespie, *The Spanish Socialist Party: A History of Factionalism*, (Oxford: Oxford University Press, 1989); and Richard S. Fischer, "The Spanish Left: Resurgence after Four Decades of Franco," Western Societies Program, Occasional Papers, no. 11 (Ithaca, N.Y.: Cornell University, 1978).

20. By article 113 of the Spanish Constitution, votes of no confidence must be sponsored by at least one-tenth of the parliament and must include the nomination of an alternate prime minister. Defeated signatories cannot present a new vote until the next session. Article 113 is intended to avoid the risk of the types of government crises that plagued the Second Republic. See Carr and Fusi, *Spain: Dictatorship to Democracy*, pp. 243–245.

21. On the Spanish Constitution, see Oscar Alzaga, *Comentario sistemático a la constitución Española de 1978* (Madrid: Ediciones del Foro, 1978). For an excellent overview, see José Maravall, *The Transition to Democracy in Spain* (New York: St. Martin's Press, 1982); Andrea Bonime-Blanc, *Spain's Transition to Democracy: The Politics of Constitution Making* (Boulder: Westview Press, 1987); and George E. Glos, "The New Spanish Constitution: Comments and Full Text," *Hastings Constitutional Law Quarterly*, vol. 7 (Fall 1979), pp. 47–128. See also the interesting discussion of the Constitution of 1978 by Manuel Fraga Iribarne, in José L. Cagigao, John Crispin, and Enrique Pupo Walker, *Spain 1975–1980: The Conflicts and Achievements of Democracy* (Madrid: Ediciones José Porrúa Terranzas, 1992) pp. 143–57.

22. On the role of the church, see Norman Cooper, "The Church: From Crusades to Christianity," in Paul Preston, ed., *Spain in Crisis* (New York: Harper & Row, 1976). On the role of the Communist party, see Eusebio Mujal Leon, *Communism and Political Change in Spain* (Bloomington: Indiana University Press, 1983); and Congressional Research Service, *A Report on West European Communist Parties* (Washington, D.C., 1977).

23. See Raymond Carr, *Modern Spain, 1875–1980* (Oxford: Oxford University Press, 1980). Also, for a brief overview of the Franco legacy, see Edward Malefakis, "Spain and the Francoist

Heritage," in John H. Herz, ed., *From Dictatorship to Democracy: Coping with the Legacies of Authoritarianism and Totalitarianism* (Westport, Conn.: Greenwood Press, 1982), pp. 215–230.

24. See Kenneth Maxwell, ed., *Spanish Foreign and Defense Policy* (Boulder, Colo.: Westview Press, 1991); Carolyn P. Boyd and James M. Boyden, "The Armed Forces and the Transition to Democracy in Spain," in Thomas D. Lancaster and Gary Prevost, eds., *Politics and Change in Spain* (New York: Praeger, 1985); and Kenneth Medhurst, "Spain's Evolutionary Pathway from Dictatorship to Democracy," *West European Politics*, vol. 7, no. 2 (April 1984), pp. 30–50.

25. See Antonio Sánchez-Gijón, *El gasto de defensa y el gasto militar en España 1975–1982* (Madrid: Instituto de Cuestiones Internacionales, 1982). See also the comprehensive analysis by José Antonio Olmeda Gómez, *Las Fuerzas Armadas en el Estado Franquista: 1939–1975* (Madrid: Ediciones el Arquero, 1988).

26. Francisco Oriza, *Juventud Española 1984* (Madrid: Ediciones S.M., 1985), p. 406.

27. On nationalities within Spain, see Robert P. Clark, *The Basques: The Franco Years and Beyond* (Reno, Nev.: University of Nevada Press, 1979); and "Dimensions of Basque Political Culture in Post-Franco Spain," in William A. Douglass, ed., *Basque Politics: A Case Study in Ethnic Nationalism*, Basque Studies Program Occasional Papers Series, no. 2 (Reno, Nev.: University of Nevada Press, 1985); Norman L. Jones, "The Catalan Question since the Civil War," in Preston, *Spain in Crisis*, pp. 239–241; Stanley G. Payne, "Catalan and Basque Nationalism," *Contemporary History*, vol. 6, no. 1 (1979); Stanley G. Payne, *Basque Nationalism* (Reno, Nev.: University of Nevada Press, 1975); Kenneth Medhurst, "Basques and Basque Nationalism," in Colin Williams, ed., *National Separatism* (Vancouver: University of British Columbia Press, 1982); and Francisco J. Llera, "Conflicto en Euskadi Revisited," in Richard Gunther, ed., *Politics, Society, and Democracy: The Case of Spain* (Boulder, Colo.: Westview Press, 1993), pp. 169–195.

28. See the discussion by Jean-Jacques Kourliandsky, "Espagne l'espoir?" *Esprit* (Paris), February 1983, pp. 73–86.

29. See Maravall, *The Transition*, pp. 7–8. See also C. Moya, *El poder económico en España* (Madrid: Túcar, 1975).

30. This is a point Peter McDonough and Antonio López Pina stress repeatedly in their various writings. See, for instance, their "Perceptions of the Post-Authoritarian Cortes: Spain in

Comparative Perspective" (paper for the Conference on Parliaments, Policy, and Regime Support, Durham, N. C., December 2–5, 1982). See also Peter McDonough, Antonio López Pina, and Samuel H. Barnes, "The Spanish Public in Political Transition," *British Journal of Political Science*, vol. 11 (1981), pp. 49–79.

31. For a discussion of the church's role in Spain in relation to the political parties, which is more comprehensive than its title implies, see Eusebio Mujal-León, "The Left and the Catholic Question in Spain," *Western European Politics*, vol. 5 (April 1982), pp. 32–54; see also Laurent Boetsch, "The Church in Spanish Politics," in Lancaster and Prevost, *Politics and Change in Spain*, pp. 144–67; and Audrey Brassloff, "The Church and Post-Franco Society," in Christopher Abel and Nissa Torrents, eds., *Spain: Conditional Democracy* (New York: St. Martin's Press, 1984).

32. The verdict of the court martial was announced in June 1982. The two leaders received thirty-year sentences; but twelve of those on trial were absolved, and twenty others received light sentences. Colonel Tejero, who led the assault on parliament, had in 1978 received a merely symbolic sentence for a previous coup conspiracy.

33. Capt. Juan Milans del Bosch, son of the general who had been the only regional commander to mobilize his troops in response to the seizure of parliament (Lt. Gen. Milans del Bosch of the Valencia garrison), had called the king "useless" and "a pig" in public and was given a light reprimand in October 1981.

34. For a comprehensive analysis of elections and party formations prior to 1992, see Michael Buse, *La Nueva Democracia Española: Sistema de partidos y Orientación del Voto (1970–1983)* (Madrid: Unión Editorial, 1984). This book, like several excellent analyses of the evolving Spanish political system, was sponsored by the Friedrich Naumann Foundation.

35. There is now a very large body of writing on the transitional period in Spain. Among the best works in English are José María Maravall and Julián Santamaría, "Political Change in Spain and the Prospects for Democracy," in Guillermo O'Donnell, Philippe C. Schmitter, and Laurence Whitehead, eds., *Transitions from Authoritarian Rule: Southern Europe* (Baltimore, Maryland: Johns Hopkins University Press, 1986), pp. 71–108; Beate Kohler, *Political Forces in Spain, Greece and Portugal* (London: Butterworth Scientific, 1982), pp. 3–91; and Richard Gunther, "Spain: The Very Model of the Modern Elite Settlement," in John Higley and Richard Gunther, *Elites and Democratic Consolidation: Latin America and Southern Europe*

(Cambridge: Cambridge University Press, 1992). Interestingly, almost all the work by foreigners on Spain's democratic transformation has been strongly comparative in its intellectual framework.

36. See Gunther, Sani, and Shabad, *Spain after Franco;* and Lancaster and Prevost, *Politics and Change in Spain.* For further discussion of election returns in Spain, see Linz, "Europe's Southern Frontier;" Jonathan Marcus, "The Triumph of Spanish Socialism: The 1982 Elections," *Western European Politics*, vol. 6, no. 3 (July 1983), pp. 281–86; and the 1977, 1979, and 1982 editions of Howard Penniman and Eusebio Mujal-León, *Spain at the Polls* (Durham, N.C.: Duke University Press).

37. For a good description of the roles played by González and Guerra in renovating the PSOE, see Gilmour, *The Transformation of Spain*, pp. 102–104. Richard Gunther provides a detailed analysis of the transformation of the PSOE from opposition to governing party in Stanley G. Payne, ed., *The Politics of Democratic Spain* (Chicago: Chicago Council on Foreign Relations, 1986), pp. 8–49.

38. For more on Spanish communism, see Eusebio Mujal-León, *Communism and Political Change in Spain* (Bloomington: Indiana University Press, 1983); and "Decline and Fall of Spanish Communism," *Problems of Communism*, vol. 35 (March/April 1986), pp. 1–27.

39. For an excellent and comprehensive bibliography of the extensive literature on the 1980s, see José Antonio Diaz Martinez, "Selección de Bibliografiá sobre la Decada del Cambio en España (1982–1992)," in Alfonso Guerra and José Felix Tezanos, eds., *La Decada del Cambio: Diez Años de Gobierno Socialista, 1982–1992* (Madrid: Editorial Sistema, 1992), pp. 737–79.

40. Rafael Bañón-Martinez, "Spanish Military Reform and Modernization," in Kenneth Maxwell, *Spanish Foreign and Defense Policy*, pp. 238–61; and Stanley G. Payne, "Modernization of the Armed Forces," in Payne, *The Politics of Democratic Spain*, pp. 181–96.

41. Maxwell, *Spanish Foreign and Defense Policy*, p. 12.

42. See Angel Viñas, *Los Pactos Secretos de Franco con Estados Unidos* (Barcelona: Grijalbo, 1981).

43. For a discussion of some indications of the role of the West Europeans, especially the West Germans, in both Spain and Portugal, working through their "political" foundations, see Beate Kohler, *Political Forces in Spain, Greece and Portugal* (London: Butterworth, 1982).

44. On moral and financial backing for the PSOE from the Socialist International, see Gilmour, *The Transformation of Spain*, pp. 165–67.

45. Wells Stabler, comments made at the Foreign Policy Center Conference on Democratization, Foreign Service Institute, U.S. Department of State, 1986, an edited version of which was published in Hans Binnendijk, ed., *Authoritarian Regimes in Transition* (Washington, D.C.: Center for the Study of Foreign Affairs, Foreign Service Institute, U.S. Department of State, 1987). According to David Gilmour, American secretary of state Henry Kissinger had been opposed to the legalization of the PCE. See Gilmour, *The Transformation of Spain*, p. 174.

46. See Javier Rupérez, "Spain, the United States, and NATO: Political and Strategic Dilemmas," in Joyce Lasky Shub and Raymond Carr, eds., *Spain: Studies in Political Security* (New York: Praeger, 1985), pp. 13–20; Benny Pollack, *The Paradox of Spanish Foreign Policy* (New York: St. Martin's Press, 1987); Gregory F. Treverton, *Spain: Domestic Politics and Security Policy*, Adelphi Papers (London: International Institute for Strategic Studies, 1986), no. 204; and Angel Viñas, "Spain, the United States, and NATO," in Abel and Torrents, *Spain: Conditional Democracy*, pp. 40–58.

47. See comprehensive poll results in "El 52% de los Españoles es contrario a la permanencia de España en la OTAN," *El Pais*, October 28, 1984, p. 1.

48. *El Pais*, May 6, 1985.

49. For a wide-ranging Spanish overview of Spain's role in NATO, see Antonio Garriques y Díaz-Cañabote, Rafael Luis Bardojí, et al, *España dentro de la Alianza Atlantica*, (Madrid: Instituto de Cuestiones Internacionales, 1988).

50. Cited in Donald Share, *Dilemmas of Social Democracy: The Spanish Socialist Workers' Party in the 1980s* (New York: Greenwood Press, 1989), p. 79.

51. See Victor Alba, "Spain's Entry into NATO," in Lawrence S. Kaplan, Robert W. Clawson, and Raimondo Luraghi, eds., *NATO and the Mediterranean* (Wilmington, Del.: Scholarly Resources, 1985); Pollack, *The Paradox of Spanish Foreign Policy;* Carlos Robles Piquer, "Spain in NATO: An Unusual Kind of Participation," *Atlantic Community Quarterly*, vol. 24, no. 4 (Winter 1986/87), pp. 325–30; and Richard Gillespie, "Spain's Referendum on NATO," *Western European Politics*, vol. 9, no. 4 (October 1986), pp. 238–44. The referendum stated:

"The Government considers it in the national interest that Spain remain in the Atlantic Alliance and resolves that established on the following terms:

1. The participation of Spain in the Atlantic Alliance will not include its incorporation in the integrated military structure.
2. The prohibition on the deployment, storage or introduction of nuclear arms on Spanish territory will be continued.

3. The United States military presence in Spain will be gradually reduced.

Do you consider it advisable for Spain to remain in the Atlantic Alliance according to the terms set forth by the Government of the nation?"

See *Revista de Estudios Internacionales*, vol. 7, no. 1 (January–March 1986).

Spain's anti-nuclear sentiment is partially the result of a 1966 accident in which an American strategic bomber accidentally dropped four hydrogen bombs into the ocean near southeastern Spain. This accident, according to former U.S. Ambassador Angier Biddle Duke, created a long-term distrust of atomic weaponry. From remarks by Angier Biddle Duke, "Spain: A Personal Perspective," at the World Affairs Council, Boston, Mass., February 25, 1993.

52. See Richard F. Grimmett, *U.S.-Spanish Bases Agreement* (Washington, D.C.: Congressional Research Service, Library of Congress, 1988).

53. See Felipe González, "A New International Role for a Modernizing Spain," in Clark and Haltzel, *Spain in the 1980s*, p. 189.

54. Cited by Paul Preston and Dennis Smyth, *Spain, the EEC, and NATO*, Chatham House Paper no. 22 (London: Routledge, 1984), p. 24.

55. The use of the idea of Europe as a vehicle for democratization is well described by the former Spanish foreign minister Fernando Morán in his *Una politica exterior para España* (Barcelona: Editorial Planeta, 1981). For a good discussion of public opinion responses to foreign policy issues in Spain, see Eusebio Mujal-León, "Spain: Generational Perspectives on Foreign Policy," in Stephen Szabo, ed., *The Successor Generation* (London: Butterworth, 1983), pp. 129–35. For an overview of Spain's relations with the EC, see Pollack, *The Paradox of Spanish Foreign Policy*, pp. 129–48. On Spanish public opinion toward the EC, see Rafael López Pintor, *La Opinión Publica Española: del*

Franquismo a la Democracia (Madrid: Centro de Investigaciones Sociales, 1982); and "En Torno a las Connexiones entre Opinion Publica y Decision Politica: la Actitud de Españoles ante la Communidad Económica Europea," *Revista Española de la Opinion Publica*, no. 37 (July-September 1979).

56. Edward Moxon-Browne, *Political Change in Spain* (London: Routledge Press, 1989), p. 96.

57. The complexity and breadth of the transition agreements is highlighted by the fact that the official text of the accession agreements for Spain and Portugal covers three volumes. For a concise overview see Commission of the European Communities, Memo 169/85 (Brussels: Commission of the European Community, December 20, 1985); Alfred Tovias, *Foreign Economic Relations of the European Community: The Impact of Spain and Portugal* (Boulder, Colo.: Lynne Rienner Publishers, 1990); and Browne, *Political Change in Spain*, pp. 95–99.

58. Oscar Bajo and Angel Torres, "El Commercio Exterior y la Inversion Extranjera Directa tras la Integracion de España en la CE," in Viñals, ed., *La Economîa Española ante el Mercado Unico Europeo: Las Claves del Proceso de Integración* (Madrid: Alianza Editorial, 1992), pp. 169 and 201.

59. Felipe González, "A New International Role for a Modernizing Spain," in Clark and Haltzel, *Spain in the 1980s*, p. 185.

60. While most observers considered this a successful outcome for González, the conservative opposition party, Partido Popular, in criticism that was self-contradicting, attacked González for appearing as a beggar and for not obtaining greater funding.

61. The European currency unit (ECU) is the unit of accounting for the European Monetary System. The value of the ECU is determined by the value of a basket of currencies of all EC member states, and its relationship to the dollar fluctuates according to the value of currencies in international markets.

62. Reuters, March 20, 1991.

63. The Moncloa Pacts, signed by the governing UCD and the major political parties, set a ceiling on wage increases in exchange for a government promise to lower inflation and a commitment to introduce an array of economic measures including tax reform and changes to social security, housing, urbanization, monetary, and energy policy. Though lacking direct participation by the unions and employers' organization, these pacts established a pattern of tripartite negotiations among the government, employers, and unions to be followed in the subsequent agreements. The Inter-Confederation Framework Agreement signed by the UGT and CEOE revised the Moncloa pay guidelines and instituted a framework for reducing working

hours, banning overtime, and increasing productivity. The National Employment Agreements signed by the government, the UGT, CCOO, and CEOE, established new pay norms and a government promise to boost employment and reform social security. The Social and Economic Agreement, signed by the Socialist government, UGT, and CEOE, was the broadest of the agreements. The agreement included government commitments to job creation, job training, and health and safety measures at work, and a legally binding contract between labor and employers regarding wages and productivity.

64. See Joseph Harrison, *The Spanish Economy in the Twentieth Century* (New York: St. Martin's Press, 1985; and Paul Preston, *The Triumph of Democracy in Spain* (New York: Methuen, 1986).

65. Loukas Tsoukalis, *The New European Economy* (Oxford: Oxford University Press, 1993), p. 259.

66. For a comprehensive and critical analysis of the PSOE's first two terms in office, see Donald Share, *Dilemmas of Social Democracy: The Spanish Socialist Workers' Party in the 1980s*.

67. Economist, April 25, 1992.

68. For the development of the Socialist government's policy toward Latin America, see Tomás Mestre Vives, *La Politica Iberoamericana del Gobierno Socialista Español* (Madrid: Instituto de Cuestiones Internacionales, 1985). And for the development of policy through 1990, see Antonio Marquin, "Spanish Foreign and Defense Policy since Democratization," and Carlos A. Zaldivar, "Spain in Quest of Autonomy and Security: the Policies of the Socialist Government 1982–1990," in Maxwell, *Spanish Foreign and Defense Policy*, pp. 19–62 and pp. 187–213.

69. See Joaquín Roy, ed., *The Reconstruction of Central America: The Role of the European Community* (Miami, Fla.: University of Miami North-South Center, 1992).

70. For a detailed overview of foreign policy under the Socialists, see Juan Antonio Yañez-Barnuevo and Angel Viñas, "Diez años de política exterior del gobierno socialista (1982–1992)," in Alfonso Guerra and Jose Felix Tezanos, eds., *La Decada del Cambio: Diez Años de Gobierno Socialista (1982–1992)* (Madrid: Editorial Sistema, 1993), pp. 85–134; and Benny Pollack, *The Paradox of Spanish Foreign Policy* (New York: St. Martins Press, 1987).

71. For a detailed discussion of the history of Spain's relations with Israel and the Arab world, see Pollack, *The Paradox of Spanish Foreign Policy*, pp. 93–101.

72. Fernando Morán's resignation as Minister of Foreign Affairs in July 1985 and his replacement by Francisco Fernandez Ordoñez marked the abandonment of the PSOE policy of "Third World-ism." See Donald Share, *Dilemmas of Social Democracy*, p. 68.

73. Within weeks of establishing relations with Israel, Spain upgraded the diplomatic status of the representation of the Palestinian Liberation Organization (PLO) in Madrid to the ambassadorial level. Consequently, Spain is one of the few European countries to maintain official relations with both Israel and the PLO, a fact that facilitated its ability to host the Middle East peace negotiations. See Yañez-Barnuevo and Viñas, "Diez años de política exterior del gobierno socialista (1982–1992)," in Alfonso Guerra and Jose Felix Tezanos, eds., *La Decada del Cambio: Diez Años de Gobierno Socialista (1982–1992)*, pp. 107–109.

74. Reuters, March 20, 1991.

75. Ian O. Lesser, *Mediterranean Security: New Perspectives and Implications for U.S. Policy*, (Santa Monica, Calif.: Rand, 1992), p. 39. Spain's role in controlling the Strait of Gibraltar brings to the fore the unresolved question of sovereignty over Gibraltar. While this continues to be an important issue in Anglo-Spanish relations, Spain and Great Britain have acted in recent years to decrease the level of tension over this dispute. See Moxon-Browne, *Political Change in Spain*, pp. 91–95.

76. Spain participates in the Independent European Program Group; the Conference of National Armaments Directors; the NATO Industrial Advisory Group; Advisory Group for Aerospace Research and Development; NATO Training Group; Military Agency for Standardization; NATO Electronic Warfare Advisory Committee; Military Committee Meteorological Group; and the NATO Defense College. See Angel Viñas, "Spain and NATO: Internal Debate and External Challenges," in John Chipman, ed., *NATO's Southern Allies: Internal and External Challenges* (Routledge, 1988), pp. 140–194, and Pollack, *The Paradox of Spanish Foreign Policy*, p. 171.

77. Tom Burns, "Bosnian Test for Spanish Troops: Madrid displays a fresh commitment to western security," *Financial Times*, October 27, 1992, p. 3.

78. Richard Gunther, "Spain and Portugal," in Gerald A. Dorfman and Peter J. Duignan, *Politics in Western Europe* (Palo Alto, Calif.: Hoover Institution Press, 1991), pp. 214–64. Cited on p. 249.

79. Juan Guerra, the younger brother of Alfonso Guerra—former Socialist Deputy Prime Minister and arguably the second most powerful politician in Spain following Felipe González—was

provided an office in the government building in Seville from which he exploited his family connections to pursue lucrative business ventures. Juan Guerra was charged with influence peddling and tax evasion. The scandal eventually forced the resignation of Alfonso Guerra as deputy prime minister, but he retained his position as deputy secretary of the PSOE. For a critical review of all aspects of the Socialists' ten years in power, see Javier Tusell and Justino Sinova, eds., *La Decada Socialista: El Ocaso de Felipe González* (Madrid: Espasa-Calpe, 1991).

80. Statistics obtained from OECD, *Economic Surveys: Spain 1992–93* (Paris: Organization for Economic Cooperation and Development, 1993).

81. See "World Competitiveness Scoreboard," *Los Angeles Times*, July 20, 1993, p. H6.

82. OECD, *Economic Surveys: Spain 1992–93*, p. 25.

83. For a comprehensive and theoretical analysis of the impact of EC membership on the Spanish economy, see Jose Viñals et al., "Spain and the 'EC cum 1992' Shock," in Christopher Bliss and Jorge Braga de Macedo, eds., *Unity with Diversity in the European Economy: The Community's Southern Frontier* (Cambridge: Cambridge University Press, 1990), pp. 145–234.

84. Juan Ramon Cuadrado, Guillermo de la Dehesa, and Andres Precedo, "Regional Imbalances and Government Compensatory Financial Flows: The Case of Spain," in A. Giovannini, ed., *Finance and Development: Issues and Experience* (Cambridge: Cambridge University Press 1993), p. 271.

85. This Spanish version of federalism differs from more traditional models because "not only has each region been free to decide whether or not to request autonomous status, but it has been, and will be, able to decide on the level of autonomy required" See Peter J. Donaghy and Michael T. Newton, *Spain: A Guide to Political and Economic Institutions*, (Cambridge: Cambridge University Press, 1987) p. 112.

86. The "historic regions" whose autonomous status predates the Spanish Civil War include Galicia, in addition to the Basque Country and Catalonia. For complex political and historical reasons, Galicia and Navarre did not immediately attain autonomy. See Jordi Solé Tura, *Nacionalidades y Nacionalismos en España* (Madrid: Alianza, 1985).

87. See Eduardo Lopez-Aranguren and Manuel Garcia Ferranco, "Nacionalismo y Regionalismo en la España de las Autonomias," in José Vidal-Beneyto, *España a Debate*, vol. 2, pp. 115–36. The implementation of nationalist policies can, of course, provoke strong reactions within the autonomous religions. In Catalonia, for example, where there has been wide-

spread immigration from southern Spain, the imposition of Catalan-only classes in primary schools has been appealed to the Supreme Court in Madrid. See Alan Riding, "Swords Drawn in Spain Over Teaching in Spanish," *New York Times*, November 23, 1993, p. A4.

88. OECD, *Economic Surveys: Spain 1992–93*, p. 66.
89. Ibid., p. 70.
90. It is predicted that before the end of the decade there will be as many civil servants working for regional governments as the central government. Victor M. Perez-Diaz, *The Return of Civil Society: The Emergence of Democratic Spain* (Cambridge, Mass.: Harvard University Press, 1993), p. 211.
91. Ibid., p. 205.
92. Robert P. Clark, "The Question of Regional Autonomy in Spain's Democratic Transition," in Clark and Haltzel, eds., *Spain in the 1980s*, p. 155.
93. However, the government has channeled considerable funding to poorer regions for infrastructure projects such as construction and expansion of highways, roads, and schools, which should enhance economic growth in these regions over the long run.
94. Cuadrado, de la Dehesa, and Precedo, "Regional Imbalances," p. 289.
95. Indeed, Catalonia and Madrid alone received over two-thirds of all foreign investment between 1986 and 1989. On average, during this period, Madrid received 40 percent of all foreign investment and Catalonia 27 percent. Ibid., p. 287.
96. See Vidal-Beneyto, *España a Debata*, vol. 2, p. 132.
97. Andalusia, not coincidentally, is a bastion of Socialist support and is the home of Prime Minister González and other leading politicians.
98. Caudrado, de la Dehesa, and Precedo, "Regional Imbalances," p. 288.
99. OECD, *Economic Surveys: Spain 1992–93*, p. 79.
100. For a detailed discussion of the 1992 defense directive, see Jérôme Pellistrandi, "L'Espagne Militaire en 1992," *Defense Nationale*, vol. 48. (December 1992), pp. 99–107.
101. See Howard J. Wiarda, ed., *The Iberian–Latin American Connection: Implications for U.S. Foreign Policy* (Boulder, Colo.: Westview, 1986).
102. Perez-Diaz, *The Return to Civil Society*, p. 211.
103. OECD, *Economic Survey of Spain: 1992–1993*, p. 21.
104. *Financial Times*, June 23, 1993, section 3, p. 5.

105. See José Juan Toharia, "La Situacion Demografica: Principales Rasgos y Pautas," in Jose Vidal-Beneyto, ed., *España a Debate* (Madrid: Editorial Tecnos, 1991), vol. 2, pp. 1–16.

106. See Javier Solana Madariaga, "La Educación en España en el Decenio 1982–1992," in Guerra and Tezanos, *La Decada Socialista*, pp. 351–80; and González-Anleo, "La Enseñanza en España: El Desafio de las Noventa," in Vidal-Beneyto, *España a Debate*, vol. 2, pp. 137–54.

107. See González-Anleo, "La Enseñanza en España"; and Jose Juan Toharia, "La Sociedad: La Vieja y la Nueva España," in Tusell and Sinova, *La Decada Socialista*, pp. 67–76.

108. Over the period 1985–1990, wages rose an average of 8.2 percent per annum while consumer prices rose on average 6.5 percent per annum. See table on Basic Statistics, International Comparisons in OECD, *Economic Survey of Spain: 1992–1993*.

109. Ibid. p. 24.

110. See Moxon-Browne, *Political Change in Spain*, p. 21.

INDEX

Abortion, legalization, 28
Abraham Lincoln Brigade, 35
Accession agreement, 39–40
Agriculture: Common Agriculture Policy, 39–40; population engaged in, 6; transportation of products, 39
Alfonso XIII, 12
Alianza Popular, 24, 59
Andalusia: government assistance, 80; nationalism, 76–77; Partido Popular, 66
Angola, 54, 56
Anguita, Julio, 61
Anticommunism: of Franco, 6; Iberian, 33
AP. *See* Alianza Popular
Arab-Israeli peace talks, 54
Arab Union of the Maghreb, 58
Arabs: relationship with Spain, 54–55
Ardanza, José Antonio, 74
Argentaria, 91
Armed forces. *See* Army; Military
Army: officers, reductions in numbers of, 30–31
Arzallus, Xavier, 61
Atlantic Alliance, 37, 53
Autonomy, 20–24, 49, 73–78

Axis: defeat of, 1945, 6
Aznar, José María, 59

Balkans, 95
Banco Bilbao Vizcaya, 63
Banco Central, 63
Bank of Spain, 2
Banks: and industry, 21–22
Barcelona: Olympic Games, 63, 72; rally for democracy, 18
Basque Nation and Liberty (ETA), 16–17, 61, 93–94
Basque provinces: autonomy, 62 (table), 75–76; and Constitution of 1978, 13; elections, 26, 60; Euskera language, 74; nationalism, 5, 20; nationalist party, 61, 66; Partido Nacionalista Vasco, 67; population, 49; radical party, 42; terrorism, threat of, 18–19; unassimilated nationalities, 49
Basque Socialist party, 74
Batasuna, Herri, 61
Behavioral patterns, 8
Borbón, Juan Carlos de, *See* Carlos, Juan
Bosch, Milans del, 17
Bosnia: Spanish military units

117